The Sydney Opera House

The Sydney Opera House

Vincent Smith

SUMMIT BOOKS
Published by Paul Hamlyn Pty Limited
Sydney · Auckland · London · New York

Acknowledgements

We wish to pay special thanks to Qantas Airways,
The Australian Opera, and John Fairfax and Sons Ltd
for helping us to illustrate this book so profusely
and splendidly. Ably assisting them were Reg
Morrison and John Walsh.
The book was designed by Bruno Grasswill.

Summit Books
Published by Paul Hamlyn Pty Limited
176 South Creek Road, Dee Why West, NSW, Australia 2099
First published 1974
2nd Impression 1977
First published as a Summit Softie 1979
© Copyright Paul Hamlyn Pty Limited 1974
Produced in Australia by the Publisher
Typeset in Australia by David Graphic Typesetting
Printed in Hong Kong

**National Library of Australia
Cataloguing-in-Publication Data**

Smith, Vincent.
    The Sydney Opera House.

    ISBN 0 7271 0233 8

    1. Sydney Opera House. I. Title.

725.822' 0994' 4 (1)

Contents

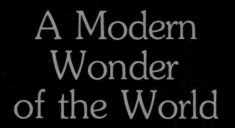

A Modern Wonder of the World

A busy Sunday afternoon.

Soaring out of the waters of Sydney Harbour at Bennelong Point is one of the world's modern architectural wonders — the Sydney Opera House, a glistening white giant which has been likened to the Taj Mahal and the Pyramids.

In terms of architectural vision and structural ingenuity these are fair analogies.

The design was always far ahead of the technology available to execute it. Almost everything about the Opera House is custom designed and built.

It has been almost 20 years in the making and has cost well over $100 million.

It has wrought a human pattern: a melodramatic outpouring of emotional controversy; sweat and tears and slogging work in the face of much cynicism; triumphs and shattering disappointments; battles and bickering between governments, designers, builders and the public; firm friends and bitter enemies.

A government fell largely because of it; the architect, Joern Utzon, resigned and was replaced by a committee which reversed the original design; its bizarre source of funds led to a tragic kidnapping and murder; as costs rose from a first wild estimate of $7 million to a rough final figure of more than $100 million; millions of dollars worth of equipment and research was merely discarded as unsuitable.

And yet it stands, between one of the world's great harbours and a bustling business district — a functional cultural monument in a city which is overwhelmingly more concerned with boating on the harbour, sports and other forms of hedonism.

The Opera House is misnamed. It was wrongly named on November 30, 1954, when the then Premier of the State of New South Wales, Mr John Joseph Cahill, announced that a committee had been appointed to advise his government on the building of "an opera house" for Sydney. The misnomer just stuck — though the building was never intended to be a mere opera house.

It was misnamed because, if nothing else, this vast cultural complex is versatile. It provides a permanent home for Sydney's performing arts.

Inside you may see a concert by a symphony orchestra or an acid rock group; hear an organ recital or a poetry reading; see opera, ballet, drama, light musicals and movies; attend lectures and conventions, public and private meetings, even religious services.

You may dine in style or eat a swift self-service meal (indoors or outdoors with a sweeping view of the Harbour); go to a cocktail party or a banquet; see an art exhibition or go to a trade fair; buy posters, books, scripts, records and sheet music. Or you may just walk and enjoy the view of the Harbour.

There are five main performance halls, two large rehearsal halls, many smaller rehearsal rooms, a cinema and chamber music hall, a large exhibition area, luxurious dressing rooms and a performers' lounge, restaurants and reception areas, administrative offices.

All this is housed under the giant shells of white and surrounded by a broad granite walkway on the water's edge.

The Opera House stands on what is probably the best site in the world for such a building, surrounded on three sides by water and on the fourth by green lawns and trees.

It faces a narrow channel of the Harbour through which the world's ships pass.

It faces the monster framework of Sydney's famous coathanger Harbour Bridge.

It faces Sydney Cove, the inlet where the Australian nation was born and which is now a busy ferry terminal and overseas passenger terminal.

It faces Farm Cove where the first food was grown for the infant colony.

It faces the gardens of historic Government House and the Botanical Gardens.

It faces a narrow arm of the city's main business district and is a neighbour of another building which was an earlier architectural revolutionary, Unilever House, one of the first curtain-wall office buildings in Sydney.

Walk towards the Opera House — through the Botanical Gardens, or down Macquarie Street (named for an early Governor of New South Wales who did much to encourage the improvement of colonial architecture), or around Circular Quay. These three walks converge at Bennelong Point.

Here you will stand, facing north, before the Opera House. Simply put, it is a monster structure of concrete, white tiles and glass consisting of ten 'shells' standing on a concrete and granite-chip podium of four and a half acres.

Standing at the foot of the staircase of more than 300 feet — thought to be the widest in the world — and looking up towards the shells, you will see, closest to you and to the left of the complex, the separate roof shell system of the Bennelong Restaurant. Further on, the largest set of shells cover the Concert Hall. And to the right of these is the smaller roof system, housing the Opera Theatre. The rest is deep inside that massive podium.

From here you will climb the steps and enter the building through the entrance half way up, which leads into the main box office foyer where you will turn left and climb a further flight of steps to the main foyer of the Concert Hall, or turn right and climb steps to the Opera Theatre's foyer.

Alternatively you will climb all the outside steps and enter the foyers of either hall directly.

If you arrive by taxi you will drive directly into the vehicle concourse beneath those huge steps, leave your car and reach the foyer areas by climbing internal staircases. For those who cannot climb steps there are special elevators.

From the base of the podium or from inside the concourse you can walk, without climbing steps, to the smaller theatres, reception rooms and exhibition area by taking the broadwalk outside the building or passages inside.

The Podium

That massive, monolithic podium on which the great white sails stand is the very guts of the Opera House. For not only is it the base on which the soaring roofs stand, but within it lie the stages and the lowest seating of both the main auditoria, all the other performing areas, the vehicle concourse, the dressing rooms, lounges, administrative offices, workshops and plant rooms — a total of about 900 rooms.

It is, indeed, a monolith. It is built of reinforced concrete poured in situ — 125,000 tons of it reinforced with 6,000 tons of steel. The podium covers more than four acres, almost the whole of Bennelong Point itself, and extends on the eastern side beyond the original sea wall and over the Harbour.

At the southern end, nearest Government House, the podium is 312 feet wide and its maximum north-south length is 600 feet. At its highest point it is 54 feet above the broadwalk, or ground level, which is itself about 12 feet above sea level.

Much of the Opera House rests on bedrock sandstone typical of Sydney's geological structure, but around its perimeter where the rock of Bennelong Point drops sharply below sea level it is supported by 550 concrete piers, each three feet in diameter. Each of these piers was put down to bedrock which, in some cases, was more than 40 feet below the Harbour's surface. In the centre of the building, where it rests directly on bedrock, concrete footings have been used. Basements extend considerably below highwater level.

The whole of the podium and the broadwalk has been clad in specially developed pink reconstituted granite slabs. The slabs are of concrete and covered with a veneer of granite which was quarried at Tarana, about 110 miles from Sydney in the Blue Mountains. The granite was pulverised and acid etched before forming the veneer on the concrete slabs. This has given a complete uniformity of colour which would not have been possible with raw granite.

Quite naturally, the podium and its associated works had to be completed before anything else could be done with the Opera House. It was termed Stage 1 of the project. (Stage 2 was construction of the roof shells and Stage 3 was the rest of the building — including the cladding for the podium, the glass work, machinery and interior fittings.) Civil and Civic Contractors Pty Ltd of Sydney won the tender for Stage 1 with a bid of $2.7 million. Stage 1 really set the pace for things to come in terms of delay and cost escalation: it was scheduled to take two years but took four to complete and cost in the end $5.1 million.

But it also set the pace in terms of technical innovation and the pushing of known technology to the limits to meet the enormous demands of Utzon's design.

The open staircase which dominates the ground level approach to the building is said to be the widest open air staircase built in modern times. It stretches almost the whole 312 feet width of the podium at the

Bennelong Restaurant from the forecourt.

A lamp glows eerily in the cavern-like vehicle concourse.

southern end. At the top of the staircase is the broad platform which provides access to the restaurant, the concert hall and the opera theatre. This platform is also the roof to the vehicle concourse, which is 282 feet long, 150 feet wide and has a ceiling clearance of 15 feet. It provides direct access from cars to the theatre complex.

Because it was to be a vehicle concourse it was necessary to provide a large covered area (big enough for cars to turn around in) without internal supports (which would either impede vision or the movement of cars).

The engineering solution to this problem was remarkable. It consists of a 7 in thick corrugated slab designed and constructed as 50 adjacent folded beam units each 6 ft wide and up to 4 ft 6 in deep. Each span has raking flights of steps and a horizontal section which makes up, in effect, a series of continuous folded beams which change shape as they rake upwards. Single spans traverse up to 160 feet without support. Engineers say it is the largest column-free concourse in the world.

Outside the concourse, the pink granite paved steps lead up to the theatre entrances. The open paving system allows rainwater to drain between the paving slabs and be carried along the natural drainage channels which were created by the folded beam construction of the vehicle concourse ceiling.

Surrounding the central podium is the broadwalk, which is both a part of the podium and an extension of it built on to piers over the water. The broadwalk is what it says it is: it provides a wide harbourside promenade on three sides of the Opera House. On the northern section, near the opera theatre, is the outdoor self-service restaurant, a popular lunch venue for downtown Sydney office workers. The broadwalk is also the access route to the drama theatre, chamber music hall-cinema and the exhibition hall.

The Shells

Even a quick look at the complex of roof shells that stand on Bennelong Point shows that there are three separate, yet integrated, shell systems — the largest housing the concert hall, the next biggest covering the opera theatre, and in the smallest group is the Opera House's premier restaurant, the Bennelong.

The imagination, technical ingenuity and heartbreak that have gone into their construction sorely strains credulity. To begin with, the Opera House project was well and truly advanced before it was known whether the roof vaults (as the shells are technically called) could even be built. The designers and engineers were wrestling with the problem while construction of the podium, on which they would stand, was going ahead. And yet, the roof vault system was the very essence of the design which Utzon had envisioned for Bennelong Point.

Three years of painstaking work in London and Sydney and countless hours of computer time went into the development of a scheme which would enable the shells to be built. In the end it was Utzon

1. Concert Hall
2. Opera Theatre
3. Concert Hall Foyer
4. Opera Theatre Foyer
5. Bennelong Restaurant
6. Car Concourse
7. Podium Stairs
8. Self Service Restaurant
9. Glass Wall of Concert Hall
10. Exhibition Hall and Chamber Music Hall/Cinema Foyer
11. Administrative Offices
12. Drama Theatre
13. Drama Theatre Stage
14. Public Lounges
15. Harbourside Foyer
16. Rehearsal/Recording Hall
17. Control Room for Rehearsal/Recording Hall
18. Production Rehearsal Room
19. Concert Organ
20. Stage of Opera Theatre
21. Machinery
22. Scenery dock and Stage Machinery
23. Chorus Rehearsal Room
24. Production Rehearsal Room
25. Entrance to Drama Theatre.

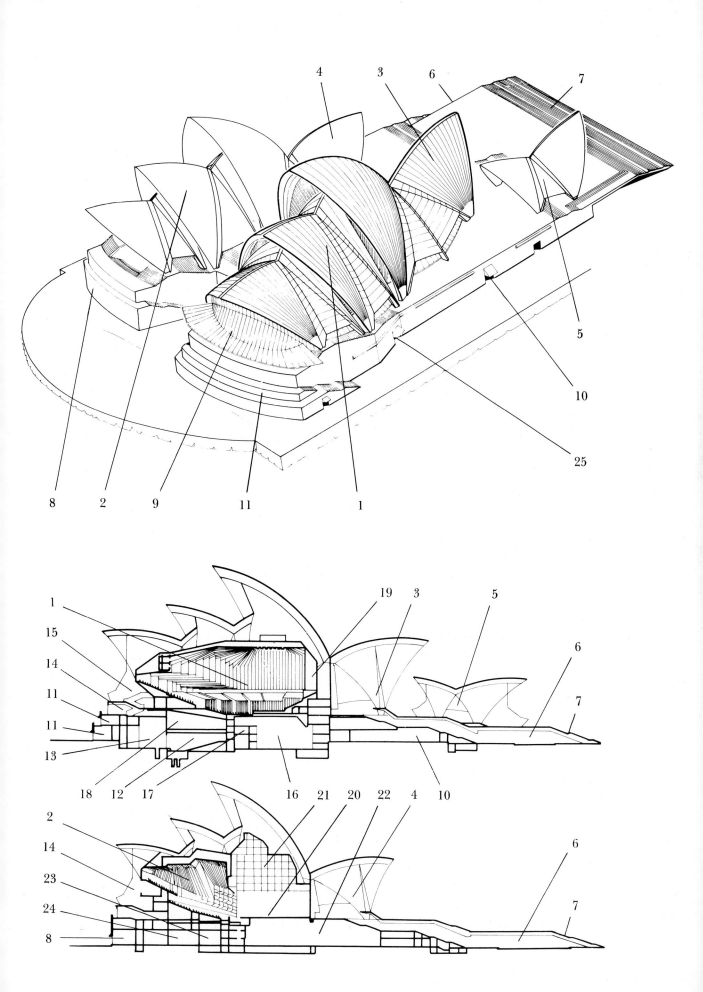

who developed the scheme by which the shells were eventually built. Every curved surface in those shells is a part of a sphere 246 feet in radius.

The biggest set of shells, those housing the concert hall, are designated A1, A2, A3 and A4, running from south to north, so that shell A1 is nearest the broad front steps of the Opera House and faces south. It is adjoined by shells A2, A3 and A4 which face north, with A4 nearest the Harbour. Correspondingly the shells covering the opera theatre are designated B1, B2, B3 and B4. The shells covering the Bennelong Restaurant are C11 (facing south) and C12 (facing north, nearest the main structure).

The tallest shell in the whole complex, A2, rises to 221 feet above sea level (which is roughly the height of a 22-storey office building) and is about 30 feet higher than the roadway of its impressive neighbour, the Sydney Harbour Bridge.

The concert hall (A series) shells run about 400 feet from south to north and at their widest span 176 feet. The opera theatre (B series) shells span 352 feet from south to north and are 128 feet at their widest point. Shell B2, the highest in the cluster, rises 186 feet above sea level.

The shell clusters are covered with a gleaming skin of more than one million white and buff ceramic tiles, made in Sweden. They cover a total area of about four acres.

The roof system is a masterpiece of prefabrication. Probably it pushes prefabrication techniques to their limits and at the same time has achieved an astonishing degree of accuracy in the assembly. The fact that the system draws on a sphere of 246 feet radius for all its component parts helped to simplify the concrete precasting.

Each roof shell consists of two opposite sets of concrete ribs, fanning out as they rise from a single point on the podium, until they meet at a centre line which is the regularly arcing peak of the shell. The structure is dramatically illustrated in the front foyers of both the concert hall and the opera theatre where no acoustic ceilings interfere with the cathedral-like effect Utzon was seeking to achieve from the exposed ribs, which form both roofs and walls of the vaults.

The ribs are Y-shaped with the stem of the Y extending into the building to create a fan or concertina effect; the tops of the Y provide the structure on which the outside skin of concrete and tiles is laid. As they rise, fanning out and curving inwards towards the centre line at the peak of each shell, the ribs taper out so that the higher they go the wider they get. This means that there is a uniform narrow gap between each rib — narrow enough to be filled with concrete to provide a sealed ceiling. In the main foyers where acoustic ceilings have not been installed, this does, in fact, become the ceiling. It is also in these areas that the segments which make up each rib can be clearly seen.

All the ribs were pre-cast on the site (just to the south west of the main steps) in plywood moulds resting on a steel framework. Each rib is made up of

The stairway.

The covered interior stairway to the Concert Hall foyer thrusts up through the glass wall hanging from the first great shell.

a number of 15 ft segments and there are 2194 separate segments in the roof system. And yet, because of the spherical geometry of the system, only four moulds were needed for the casting. In fact, ten were built to speed up the casting and some irregular segments in the peaks required custom moulding. But so swift was the casting process and so proficient did the casters become that they far outpaced the builders and many segments had to be carted from the site for storage (away from the imagination of graffiti writers) at Long Bay Jail.

Each mould was 75 ft long and thus able to cast five of the 15 ft rib segments at a time.

Three tower cranes, bought in France at a cost of $100,000 each, were used to hoist the ribs from the casting yard to the shells. To support each segment while it was being placed into position on the rib, the Hornibrook Group (contractors for Stage 2, as the construction of the shells was called) devised an ingenious erection arch. Four of these were used in the scaffolding during erection of the shells. They had a telescoping mechanism, were inclinable and traversable so that they could adjust to the size of the particular rib on which they were working.

As the erection arch brought each segment close to its position in the rib, a few inches above the one laid before it, the construction crew would use a stick or paint roller to smear Araldite epoxy resin glue on the two surfaces which were to come together. The new segment was then laid on top of the one below it and the two were thus glued together.

All the roof ribs are glued together in this way. But they are also post-stressed with steel cables — nine of them, about ½ inch thick — which run through each rib from the podium to the peak. The tops of the ribs are also cable-stressed together through the peaks of the shells to form a stable arch. There are 280 complete ribs of varying sizes in the roof system, which weighs some 28,600 tons.

One of the major difficulties encountered in erecting the ribs was their three dimensional nature and the flexibility of the ribs themselves. Mr Corbet Gore, project manager for the Hornibrook Group during Stage 2, has explained: 'The ribs are very flexible, of thin concrete, and heavily stressed. There were some deflections early, and the sheer geometry of the design made it difficult to know if the ribs were in the right place.' (Consider 280 separate segmented ribs rising independently from the ground, all of which have to meet precisely at the peak; an error close to the ground would be multiplied enormously by the time the rib reached its peak.)

Mr Gore went on: 'With Ove Arups and Partners, the consulting engineers, we developed a survey system which enabled us to overcome the deflection problem and to control the three dimensional position in space.' The ribs took three years to erect.

Outside, the roof shells are covered with a prefabricated skin of one million white ceramic tiles which were set into concrete 'lids' or slabs. The tiles come from Sweden, where they were made to order by Hoganas AB, and are in two types, one highly

glossed and almost white, the other in a flat finish and buff coloured. The two types give the roof shells their pattern and the flat finished buff tiles help to reduce the glare that would be painful were the entire surface of the shells covered in glossy material. Utzon himself selected the tiles and supervised their development with Hoganas.

He has said: 'The cover for these gigantic curved forms has the greatest influence on the visual impact. The wrong material would ruin the appearance.'

Ceramic tiles, he said, were durable, weather resistant and would age gracefully, acquiring a handsome patina. Utzon's search for the right tiles took him first to the homes of ceramics, China and Japan, where he gathered together a collection of samples which he took to Europe to study the textures, colours and glazes. Nowhere did he find a standard tile which suited his requirements so it was in consultation with Hoganas that two were developed which suited him perfectly.

Because they were so critical to the eventual appearance of his creation Utzon concerned himself intensely with the application of the tiles to the roof shells. He decided that only prefabrication could give him the uniform surface he wanted. Conventional application techniques with standard tiles would have involved scores of different workers who, though part of a team, would work independently. 'This could not possibly produce a uniform surface,' Utzon said.

On the site, the tiles (each 4¾ in square by ⅝ in thick) were laid face downwards in a mould and concrete was poured over their backs to form a slab or, as the builders termed it, a lid. The lids — there are some 4220 in the roofs measuring up to 33 feet by 7 ft 6 in and weighing four tons — were then hoisted into position by the giant cranes.

Casting the lids, which are chevron-shaped and give the skin of the Opera House a zig-zag pattern, was, like almost everything connected with the project, a complex task. Not only did they have to be curved but they had to be a segment from a sphere of radius 246 feet and they had to conform with the utmost precision with these dimensions.

But even more difficult was the task of attaching them to the roof ribs. They are attached by phosphor-bronze bolts, which had been embedded in both the ribs and the tile lids when they were cast, and aluminium-bronze brackets. This seemed a relatively simple system but it became one that caused one of the great construction crises. As the lids were being attached to the ribs it was discovered, as they reached higher up the shells, that the higher the lids went the more out of position were the bolts embedded in both the lids and the ribs. So serious was the problem that scrapping the existing lids was considered. But an almost incredibly complex system of surveying and computer calculating was devised and the brackets were redesigned to overcome the problem so that all the errors, small though they are, are concealed beneath those perfectly placed white shells.

Glass Walls

Intricacy and complexity are run-of-the-mill words when you talk of design and construction of the Opera House. But one area where they apply with fullness, even in the context of this building, is in the design and construction of the 1½ acres of glass walls which enclose the giant roof shells.

Utzon had dreamed of his soaring concrete sails, his latter day Gothic cathedral, being draped elegantly rather like a beautiful lady in a glass veil. He envisioned the glass falling in soft flowing lines, draped from the top of the shells and flowing almost to the ground where they would form the roofs of bars and lobbies on the harbour side of the building.

Like so many other aspects of the building the glass walls were conceived and a design philosophy adopted without any knowledge of whether, in fact, they could be built.

The problems of building the glass walls, along with many other problems, were revealed when Utzon's plans were unveiled in Sydney in 1957. The problem of the glass was still being struggled with by a team of engineers as late as 1967 after Utzon had resigned from the project.

Originally Utzon had in mind the use of minimal plywood mullions to which a bronze cladding had been bonded. Each of these would be stepped back and reduced in size from its neighbour to match the falling arch of the roof. These were to hang from the shells and towards the bottom they would rake forward to form the roof to the bars and lobbies.

Together they would form a coherent group of mullions which would, without the glass, appear to be the plane of the glass walls. But Utzon's idea was to have the glass spanning from the rear edge of the forward mullion to the leading edge of the next mullion back.

This would give a sort of stepped back effect to the walls' surfaces. It was essential that the mullions be of minimal size so as not to overpower the visual effect of the stepped-back glass panes falling in folds rather like a curtain.

When Utzon left, the idea had been advanced considerably but still no technique had been developed for bonding bronze on to plywood.

Experimentally, the new architects tried different material for the mullions like bronze-clad steel and pre-cast concrete, though they were still trying to preserve Utzon's concept of the flowing veil of stepped back planes. But what they achieved, when they built models, was a design which completely overpowered the glass. Except when seen directly from the front, the mullions overlapped and obscured the glass altogether, giving the effect of a solid wall supporting the shells. Utzon's draped lightness concept had disappeared, and because of this the architects abandoned the scheme.

Still trying to retain the idea of lightness, and of the glass hanging from the shells, they abandoned the idea of stepping back the mullions. Extensive work, especially with models, was carried out before the fan shape of the new concept for the walls was determined.

What's behind the glass?

17

To grasp the complexity of trying to develop the shape and structure of these walls, remember that the architects were still trying to achieve an effect of lightness, of draped glass, which fell from the shells and then began, as it neared the bottom, to push outwards in a sort of splay. It meant that almost no one shape in the whole wall was identical with another — and the area to be covered was 1½ acres.

Computers, ingeniously used, had made possible the calculations for the engineering of the main shells. They were to be used again on this enormous mathematical problem. With computers, the engineers were confident, they could calculate the dimensions of every component part so that when it came to installation the whole structure would fit together perfectly like a giant jigsaw puzzle. And no site measurements would have to be made.

The first step was to devise a structural system which would support the enormous weight of the walls and still allow the final product to look as though it had been draped from the shells. It had to allow for strength that would withstand gales howling up the harbour; it had to allow for expansion and contraction, the effects of scorching sun on such a vast expanse of glass during a Sydney summer.

In order to program the computers a system had to be devised to relate the spherical forms of the shells to the planes of the podium on which the building stood.

Once this program was devised the computers could be used to calculate the complex array of data that was needed before construction could begin: the length of every component, the angle it had to be cut at its ends, the position of the bolts, the shape at the point where it met the roof shells, the size and shape of each individual pane of glass and the various forces that would act on every component.

And if this process was complicated and puzzling — even to the experts — it was also long, drawn out and frustrating. The slightest change in calculations could mean the scrapping of a whole computer program and reworking a new one. For example, a change to allow sufficient clearance between glass and concrete shell meant the whole program had to be changed and run through the computer again. It meant long hours of painstaking work — and often many tears.

In addition, the whole thing had to come together at one time. Because almost none were identical, almost every component relied on every other to take its place in the whole scheme. This also meant that the whole scheme had to be computed and finalised before the architects could decide whether the engineers had come up with a scheme which was acceptable to the aesthetics that were sought. As in the development of the roof shells, relations between architects and engineers were often strained almost to breaking point: when the engineers were happy with a scheme they had devised and the architects rejected it on aesthetic grounds.

Despite these problems the project went ahead. In the end the engineers gave the installation

contractors — a consortium of four leading Sydney glass companies, Vetro, Astor, Sandys and O'Brien, known collectively as VASOB — more than 200 working drawings and more than 30,000 dimensions from which components were made and assembled.

It was a complicated enough project but the fact that glass was the material being worked with made it even more complicated.

Glass had to be hoisted up into position, once cut to shape, and once in position the risk of it breaking and falling had to be totally eliminated. The glass had to be able to shut out the sounds of the harbour, just as the concrete shells did. And it had to be tinted to reduce as much as possible the glare and heat created by the sun beating down on it.

A special laminated glass, which would stay in position if broken, was chosen over toughened glass, which would fall in thousands of tiny pieces if broken. The laminations would consist of two sheets of glass bonded together by a transparent synthetic rubber — each completed sheet about ¾ in thick. And it was to be tinted topaz, a colour unique to the Opera House.

The manufacturing contract went to Boussois-Souchon-Neuvesel of France, one of the few glass makers in the world which still utilises the old pot-casting process. Most modern glass manufacturing processes turn out about 400 tons of glass in one batch and this was far more than even the Sydney Opera House needed.

Once the glass had been imported to Australia it then had to be cut to size. Cutting of glass like this had never been done before and the Sydney consortium, VASOB, was commissioned to develop the saws which would do the job. This in itself, along with other research into the type of sealants that should be used and finding out the strength characteristics of the glass, took about two years.

While this was going on the designers settled for a frame system of steel mullions to which were attached bronze glazing bars; the step-back concept was abandoned in favour of single-surface walls where each pane of glass virtually abutted its neighbour.

The glass arrived in Australia by ship. At a cost of $16 a square foot it was treated almost royally in the cutting factory which had been established on the northern broadwalk, where the open air restaurant now is. The blanks of glass were cut by diamond edged circular saws to sizes ranging from about four feet square to about 14 feet by 8 ft 6 in.

Fitting began early in 1971. The steelwork had gone in with extraordinary precision and, according to one of the consulting engineers on the job, an estimated tolerance of any point being half an inch out of position proved to be pessimistic. About 2000 panes of glass in more than 700 different sizes were fitted to the Opera House.

Once cut, the glass had to be hoisted into position. Cyclone steel scaffolding was erected to provide a working platform and cut panes of glass were hoisted to the platform by one of the tower cranes.

The broadest open staircase in the world.

On the platform a unique and, naturally, specially designed machine was used to install the glass. It was a small mobile crane which used suction cups instead of hooks. Picking up a pane of glass at a time, the crane would be manhandled by the glazers into the position required, the glass was fitted into place and bedded into the silicone rubber sealant, the suction vacuum was cut and the crane released the glass to be trundled away for its next load.

The only glass to metal contact in the structure was two stainless steel studs which supported each pane in the horizontal glazing bar with the silicone rubber sealant. On each vertical edge the glass rested on a neoprene backing.

Often it took a day to install three panes of glass. In such a complex task it was remarkable and a tribute to the engineering and design of the system that each glass panel fitted precisely into the mullions. In the whole job the biggest error was a quarter inch.

The glass walls of the Opera House deserved thoroughly the Engineering Excellence Award of the Association of Consulting Engineers, Australia, the highest distinction bestowed for such work in Australia, which they won for Ove Arup and Partners in 1972.

Inside

Inside the great vaulted foyer of the concert hall Utzon's vision of a Gothic cathedral becomes a reality. From the pink granite floor, the bare grey concrete ribs arch upwards to their peak, growing wider as they rise. The ribbed and folded pattern of light and shade they create gives the impression of spare splendour.

Here there is no need for elaborate chandeliers, for deep pile carpet and gilt: the geometry, the form, the volume are themselves the splendour. This is the essence of Utzon's building — and it has been carried through by his successors — a monumental yet functional building in need of no cosmetics.

The Concert Hall

As its name implies the Concert Hall is chiefly for symphony concerts but is also available for a wide variety of purposes and has been used for conventions, fashion parades, film shows and pop concerts. It has seating for 2700 people.

It is surrounded by foyers. The front foyer is sparse, of granite, concrete and glass and is faced (behind the stage) with pink brushbox panelling with a system of geometric protrudences which break up its sheer size. There is an island bar at which guests may refresh themselves. From the front foyer, entrance passages lead around both sides of the auditorium, to the various doorways and climbing eventually to the purple carpeted harbourside foyer which is glazed to provide concert goers with the magnificent spectacle of the Harbour. In this foyer is

John Olsen's vast mural, reflecting the mood of Sydney Harbour at night. There is another bar area here, too, and balconies.

Inside the Concert Hall the eye is immediately taken by the enormous circular centre point of the ceiling, which radiates out and down to form about two-thirds of the walls. This is in white birch plywood. Suspended from this centre point are the 21 giant acrylic acoustic clouds, or rings. They are suspended over the concert platform by stainless steel cables and offer a sound reflection system which gives musicians almost instant feedback of their sound. Without them the musicians would have to wait until their music had echoed off the distant walls and ceiling.

The lower walls, stairs, floors, boxes and the stage area are panelled with the same brushbox as is used in the entrance foyer, though it is generally lighter in colour. The 2700 specially designed seats are made of the same white birch plywood which forms the ceiling and they are upholstered in magenta wool. The total stage area is 2200 square feet and apart from the lighting control panel high in the rear of the hall there are control rooms for the stage manager and broadcasts at the side of the stage beneath the boxes. Further control booths for broadcast announcers are at the sides of the lower part of the hall, beneath the boxes. There are no radial aisles and seats are reached through a number of doors. There is a translation system which can handle five languages, film and slide projection facilities and closed circuit television.

The Opera Theatre

The Opera Theatre is the second auditorium in the complex and seats 1550. Apart from opera, its use is for large drama productions and for ballet. Its foyers are virtually replicas of those in the concert hall. But inside it is vastly different and it becomes immediately obvious that the auditorium has been carefully decorated for its prime function — opera. Instead of the light, almost breezy decor of the concert hall, there is dark, almost sombre toning to the opera theatre so that there are few distractions and all audience attention is focussed on the stage.

The pleated plywood ceilings and walls are stained black, though there is some lighter colouring to the boxes which are made of concrete (there are three tiers of them on either side of the theatre). The floors are in red-brown brushbox strips. As in the concert hall, the seats are of white birch plywood, but they are upholstered in red leather.

Acoustic assistance is given by three large strip panels of acrylic which are suspended from the ceiling by steel cables. The focal point in the Opera Theatre is John Coburn's tapestry Curtain of the Sun. The stage has a total area of 4700 square feet and an acting area of 3400 square feet.

In the centre of the stage there is a giant revolve with a diameter of 47 feet and which has two built-in platforms. Also built into the stage are four 40 feet

John Olsen's mural, Salute to Slessor's Five Bells — Concert Hall foyer.

square lifts for vertical handling of stage scenery. The theatre has an entirely concealed lighting system which gives a completely blacked out effect when the house lights go down. The proscenium arch is 38 feet wide and the stage has a performing depth of 52 feet. The orchestra pit is designed for a maximum of 75 musicians and it can be raised to the stage level to provide additional performing area in the theatre.

Set storage is two levels below the stage and scene changes are carried out by machinery which is operated from consoles off stage. Control booths for the highly complex lighting system and the electronic sound and acoustic system are at the rear of the theatre. There is a three language translation system, film and slide projection and closed circuit television.

Drama Theatre

Entrance to the Drama Theatre is off the western broadwalk, into the side of the podium. It has a comfortably furnished entrance foyer which boasts a painting by the distinguished Australian, Charles Blackman (a gift of the Sony electronics company of Japan). There is a bar.

The drama theatre seats 550 and is designed for drama, though its use is also for small scale opera and ballet (the Threepenny Opera was a part of the opening season). It has a resident company, the Old Tote Theatre Company, which will occupy it for 38 weeks a year. The colour scheme is blue and red; a deep blue wool carpet and the vermilion wool upholstery of the seats, which are of the same white birch plywood used throughout the Opera House.

The ceiling is of extruded aluminium which hides its unique air conditioning system and most of the walls are of plain concrete, as cast. Some wall sections are covered with plywood. The theatre also has translation, film and slide projection systems and closed circuit television. This is the home of John Coburn's other tapestry, Curtain of the Moon. The stage has a total area of 3800 square feet and a main performing area of 2900 square feet. There is a two-piece revolve with an outer diameter of 46 feet and an inner diameter of 30 feet. There is a forestage platform which can be lowered to provide an orchestra pit for a maximum of 35 musicians. Lighting and sound control booths are behind the last row of seats.

The Music Room

This is the smallest theatre in the Opera House complex with seating for 420 and a prime use of recitals and chamber music performances. It has a dual role however and doubles as the cinema. The white birch plywood which is characteristic of the Opera House has been used extensively in the ceiling and the walls. The light grey carpet which covers the floors also extends up the rear wall, where the control booths are located. The white birch seats are covered in charcoal grey wool. The auditorium is

Custom-built seating of white birch plywood and specially ordered fabrics.

The light and the dark of the Opera Theatre.

equipped for 70 mm, 35 mm and 16 mm film projection as well as for slides. It has a three language translation system. The performing platform is 400 square feet.

Reception Hall

The Reception Hall is off the main box office foyer on the eastern side of the building and overlooks the Harbour. It is designed for special receptions, dinners and cocktail parties. It can also be used for intimate recitals. One wall is entirely of glass, one is of raw concrete and the other two are panelled in white birch plywood. The 2500 square feet of floor space are covered with an emerald green carpet.

Exhibition Hall

This is an L-shaped area of 7000 square feet which is available for trade displays as well as for art exhibitions.

Rehearsal Rooms

There are five of these in the Opera House, including special ballet and music rooms. All are fairly sparse but attractively panelled and their floors are of the same wood as is used in the main auditoria.

Recording Hall

This is the vast room left beneath the stage of the Concert Hall when the stage machinery was dismantled. It has a floor area of 6900 square feet and two levels of galleries. Primarily it is designed for recording concerts by the Sydney Symphony Orchestra but it is also used as a major rehearsal room and on Sundays it is used for hourly concerts and recitals (admission $1). It has acoustical qualities similar to the Concert Hall. Apart from boadcast facilities it is also equipped to handle direct television broadcasts.

Offices and Library

These are on the Harbour side, overlooking the broadwalk beneath the Concert Hall. They also house the Opera House's Library, the Dennis Wolanski Library of Performing Arts, which contains reference works and archives about the performing arts. It is named for the Sydney businessman and sculptor who donated $10,000 for its establishment. Special arrangements can be made for public access to the library but generally it is open to those who use the Opera House.

Restaurants

There are two restaurants: the Bennelong, which is housed under the separate small set of shells at the front of the complex, and the Harbourside, which

The Rehearsal Hall during a school performance.

Once to be a massive stage machinery well in the Concert Hall, this is now the Rehearsal and Recording Hall.

opens on to the Harbour side broadwalk, beneath the Opera Theatre. The Bennelong is a la carte and rich in tone and atmosphere. The Harbourside provides a cafeteria style of service in food and drink but it has the advantage of providing open air seating among the potted trees and sculpture on the broadwalk, virtually on the Harbour.

The Green Room

Traditionally named the Green Room as are all performers' relaxation rooms, this is furnished in vivid oranges, blues and reds. It provides comfortable seating and tables around which the professional people who use the Opera House can gather for coffee, drinks or light meals. It is located directly beneath the podium between the Concert Hall and the Opera Theatre and has its own view of the Harbour.

Acoustics

By far one of the most important, if not the most important, design considerations in the Opera House concept has been acoustics. For without the right acoustics aural performances would be dead and flat and totally unsatisfying. Sydney might as well return to the muddy echoes produced by the acoustics of its Town Hall, for so long the venue for the city's symphony concerts. Acoustic requirements in the Opera House, like so many other parts of the design and construction program, have been the centre of great controversy and argument.

But what has emerged from this is a highly satisfactory, first-class acoustics system. It took a lot of developing — by Dr Vilhelm Lassen Jordan and his son Niels, Danish acoustical designers who had to their credit before tackling the Sydney Opera House major theatres in New York (the Metropolitan Opera House), London, Denmark, Sweden, Finland, Iceland, Norway and Guatemala.

Dr Jordan says of the Sydney Opera House acoustics: 'It's the best.'

Acoustical requirements differ according to the type of theatre or hall that is being built. Concert halls for example need to be able to carry the fullest range of notes from a symphony orchestra to the back seats, with very little delay, echo or reverberation. The sound reaching the back seats must be as rich and full as the sound heard by the conductor (or as close to it as possible).

In an opera theatre the same aim must be striven for but the acoustics must be able to carry the additional sound of the singers' voices, with clarity and precision so that they can be not only heard but understood. If opera theatre acoustics were to be built into a concert hall certain instruments would rise above others; there would be a sound of competing instruments rather than one rich, full sound of a symphony orchestra working as a unit, in concert. If concert hall acoustics were built into an opera theatre, the orchestra would tend to overpower the singers and 'muddy' their voices.

A shotgun helps test the acoustics of the Opera Theatre.

One of eight specially designed electro-acoustic control panels manufactured and installed by Amalgamated Wireless (Australasia) Ltd.

One of the keys to producing the right acoustics is reverberation time — the time it takes a sound to die away to inaudibility inside the hall or theatre. In concert halls a good reverberation time is considered to be two seconds, to produce the rich fullness of orchestral works. In opera theatres a slightly shorter reverberation is desirable so that the singers' voices are not lost in reverberation.

After extensive testing Dr Jordan declared that the reverberation time in the occupied (people have an effect on the movement of sound as they act as baffles and their clothes tend to absorb it) concert hall is a near perfect two seconds. In the occupied opera theatre it is a highly desirable 1.4 seconds.

To achieve this Dr Jordan and his son overcame a power of problems. Not only did they have to produce acceptable acoustics inside the performing areas, they also had to insulate these areas from the booming sounds of ships' sirens as they left Circular Quay, not 400 yards from the Opera House.

Acoustical requirements have not quite, but almost, dictated the final shape and decor of the interiors of both the main auditoria. Their ceilings were changed to conform with the requirements of the infant science of acoustics.

Usually when building concert halls or opera theatres the acoustical requirements in the structure are determined first and the architects and builders work according to these requirements. This was not the case with the Opera House: quite the reverse in fact. The building had been designed from the outside in rather than the inside out. Dr Jordan and his son had to work within many already defined parameters.

The concert hall, for example, was to seat 2700 people and required a reverberation time of two seconds. It was too small to achieve this reverberation time. Testing on one-tenth scale models showed that the volume inside the hall had to be increased considerably if this was to be achieved. The ceiling, therefore, had to be pushed as high as possible into the roof vaults, rather than to hang in a catenary curve as conceived by Utzon. (A catenary curve is the shape a flexible material assumes when it is held at the edges and allowed to droop naturally.) And the side walls of the hall had to be changed to conform with acoustical requirements. Originally the ceiling was to have come down the side walls in a series of steps. This has been changed to a vertical drop.

What now appears as the interior surfaces of the concert hall are virtually as they were built into Dr Jordan's one-tenth scale models in which the acoustics were tested. The hard surfaces of the laminated plywood walls, ceiling and floor and the specially designed seating all help to keep sound alive in the hall (they give the sound something to 'bounce' off). And the cannon-like protrudences in the ceiling, which house air conditioning ducts and lighting, help to diffuse the sound throughout the hall. Fine tuning can be achieved by adjusting and covering various openings in the walls.

To give the orchestra and conductor an immediate feedback on their sounds, while still achieving the tonal richness for the audience, the concert hall designers have installed a series of clear perspex rings which look rather like outsized, flattened Lifesavers. These hang from the ceiling and can be raised or lowered according to the individual orchestra's requirements. What they do is quickly reflect the music back down on to the orchestra rather than let it travel all the way to the ceiling. This, in effect, gives the orchestra its own private acoustical system which does not upset the sound directed at the audience.

Acoustics in the opera theatre were developed along the same lines, so that its interior design is very much a product of Dr Jordan's models. He told a newspaper reporter as the construction of both halls neared completion: "For the benefit of good voices, you would like to see for that size of theatre a reverberation time of 1.3 seconds, which is adequate, or 1.4 seconds which is good. We thought that we could reach values between 1.1 and 1.3 — actually it looks as though we have reached 1.4."

Testing of the Opera House acoustics began early in 1973, with full scale symphony concerts attended by invited construction workers and VIPs. The music ranged widely to test all aspects of the sounds produced in the hall. Starting pistols were fired and the organ was played, sounding a single note at a time as if, as one music critic put it, the Opera House's ghosts were being laid one by one.

Sir Bernard Heinz, the distinguished Australian who conducted the Sydney Symphony Orchestra during the tests, thought the hall produced a fine, clear sound — a far cry from the muddy sound of the Sydney Town Hall. Violinist Yehudi Menuhin, who played a Bach sonata in the hall in an impromptu concert to an audience of 50, said the acoustics matched the superb external appearance of the Opera House.

In the opera theatre similar tests have met with praise for the acoustics. Sydney critic Maria Prerauer, who attended the first musical test of the opera theatre, declared: "Performers are going to love it. It's alive. It carries the voice. It makes lighter work of singing. In some theatres the vocalist feels as if he has to punch the notes through cottonwool or worse, in others that the tones happily take wing. In the Sydney opera theatre all the phrases are beautifully airborne. Even without a single piece of scenery on the stage. And audiences should love it too. Voices are going to sound marvellous here, perhaps better than anywhere else — at least from the front of the stage, which was all that was used at this first try-out."

By completion, the Opera House Trust was satisfied that acoustics had lived up to the standards indicated in those first tests.

Other tests relating to the acoustics, all of which the Opera House passed splendidly, were conducted with a helicopter hovering overhead and the P and O liner Oriana blowing its siren several times in

The Concert Hall was packed for the earliest performances.

John Walsh

John Walsh

different positions around the building to test the soundproofing. Engineers with sound meters measured the Oriana's blast at a deafening 96 decibels outside but at only 50 inside the opera theatre and the concert hall, similar to the noise level produced by low conversation.

A last word on the acoustics from Dr Jordan, who, after all, is largely responsible for them: 'I don't like to be too precise, but I'm perfectly convinced that this hall (the concert hall) will be top class by world standards. As it stands I have a feeling that most of the seats are pretty good. There are some seats not so good, mainly the seats behind the stage. They're alright for orchestra but not so good for vocalists, soloists on stage, because the singers have their backs to that part of the stage.'

Stage Lighting

Stage and auditorium lighting for the Opera House was designed and more than half of it built in Australia by the contractors, Siemen's — and its description calls for yet another superlative: it is the most elaborate stage lighting system in the land.

There are more than 250 powerful spotlights for stage lighting, large xenon follower spotlights, a xenon cyclorama light in the drama theatre and fluorescent cyclorama lighting in the opera theatre. In the opera theatre there are 200 different dimmable circuits; the drama theatre has 160, the concert hall 80, and the recording and rehearsal studio 45. Five kilowatt spotlights can be attached to most of these circuits.

Among the special effects that can be achieved with the cyclorama lighting is an almost perfect stage sky: the lighting produces a sky coloured from deep blue to grey; projectors send clouds moving across the sky and electronic flashes can simulate lightning.

A computer system records the intensity settings of up to 200 different control levels which allows completely automatic lighting of a production and also eliminates long breaks during lighting rehearsals. During such rehearsals the lighting operator notes down his settings and has only to push a button allocating a cue number to each setting, which is then memorised within the computer. Then he can set the next cue.

Whenever he wants to recall previous cues — if an earlier scene is to be re-rehearsed — he does so by punching the cue number for the particular setting required and indicating to the computer when he wants the setting to appear, say two seconds or in ten minutes.

When the producer is satisfied with the rehearsals, as far as lighting goes, the whole performance can be stored on computer tape for use whenever the performance is to be repeated. More than 15 miles of multi-core cables serve electrical connections between the control desks, the switchboard rooms and the drives.

Acoustics of the Concert Hall were tested extensively by local artists at concerts.

The Timber

In the simplest of terms the Opera House is a piece of monumental architecture with a distinct influence of what is called the New Brutalism. While it is soaring and impressive in both form and volume there is a brutal, harsh, spare element to its design. All the trappings of a rich European style opera house, highly ornamented and gilded, would have looked anachronistic inside it.

The building demands a sparse and clean interior in which, as far as possible, the bare form is itself the decor, the finish. While the new architects who took over when Utzon left tried as much as possible to keep within his design philosophy without compromising themselves or the demands of the NSW government, they had to make some fundamental changes. These changes included the switch in roles for the two major auditoria. And in fitting out the interiors according to the requirements of the government and the demands which naturally followed these requirements, such as increasing the volume inside the concert hall for acoustical reasons, they have tried to keep to the spirit of Utzon's original ideas. Utzon had planned to make extensive use of timber. Partly because of this, partly for technical requirements and partly for structural requirements, timber was chosen to play a big role in the interiors of the auditoria. Timber could provide the spare finish and yet have an understated richness to it.

What timber to use?
Acoustics demanded a dense timber and engineering requirements demanded a stable timber which could withstand kiln drying and retain a high degree of stability.

It was at this stage of their considerations that the designers chose Brushbox, a rainforest tree from the lush valleys of the New England district of northern New South Wales. Brushbox trees grow here, tall and straight and do not branch out until they open out at the top; thus they produce a handsome timber that is knot-free and has a sound, strong appearance. It is available in colours varying from a light buff to pink and darker browns and reds. It is highly suited to lamination, which was required by the designers.

The brushbox chosen was used in two ways — both as individual planks and as laminated planks comprising strips ¾ in wide glued together. Individual planks are used widely in the foyers of the main auditoria but it was in the interiors of the concert hall and opera theatre that the laminated planks, with their extraordinary versatility, came into their own. They could be curved to suit any conformity within the theatre. Wide use has been made of them both on the floors, on stairs as treads and risers, and on the walls in panelling.

More than 134,000 square feet of brushbox went into the Opera House at a contract cost of $300,000. The manufacturer, Allen Taylor and Company Ltd, processed 750,000 super feet of rough-hewn timber from which it selected 400,000 super feet. This was milled, dressed and, occasionally, engineered for the Opera House. In addition to the

Stairs and wood panelling wend their way towards the Concert Hall's Harbourside foyer.

Strange geometry in the wood panelling of the Concert Hall foyers.

brushbox, plywood was used extensively in the interiors — notably in the concert hall ceiling where the white birch plywood centrepiece spreads out to drop vertically and form the upper part of the walls. The ceiling consists of 1750 panels of this plywood in a series of complicated shapes. Ceiling contractors, Cemac Brooks Pty Ltd, developed highly accurate methods of moulding plywood for this venture. And little wonder when the requirements are considered. In places the veneer had to be matched for colour and grain over panels up to 160 feet long. Each sheet of veneer cut at the company's mill was matched against a standard and then colour coded to make sure that the sheet was used correctly when the sheets were manufactured in the Cemac Brooks factory in suburban Sydney.

Extensive use has been made of moulded plywood in the ceilings and walls of the opera theatre and the chamber music hall-cinema as well as in panelling in corridors and other general areas.

Curtain of the Sun

Curtain of the Sun is one of two curtains — the other, Curtain of the Moon, hangs in the drama theatre — costing a total of $114,000, designed by the Sydney artist John Coburn and woven by the master weavers of Aubusson, the home of tapestry, near Paris. Woven in rich and warm reds, golds, pinks and browns, Curtain of the Sun represents fire, earth, air and water and is dominated by a vast heraldic sun — a device which has become almost synonymous with the style of John Coburn, who is head of the National Art School in Sydney.

The curtain is 27 feet high and 52 feet wide; it is woven in Australian wools by the firm of Pinton Freres.

Shortly before leaving for a painting sojourn in Paris in 1969 Coburn was shown around the concrete skeleton of the Opera House by architect Peter Hall.

'I was staggered by the vastness and beauty of the Opera House, even though at the time it was just all concrete,' he recalls.

'Looking down from the back of the Opera House to the stage I could see my curtains hanging there. It just came to me in a flash.

'I went home and designed them that night. It only took an hour or so and the creative part was done. I spent the next week doing the designs in colour and then took them down to the Opera House in May, 1969, just before I left for France.'

Coburn was in France when he learned some five months later that he had won the commission to design the curtains for the Opera Theatre and Drama Theatre.

With his family, Coburn lived in Paris while the curtains were woven, commuting to the tiny village of Felletin, which is about five miles from Aubusson in the valley of the Creuse.

It was here, in the Aubusson district, that Saracen warriors first began weaving tapestries in the eighth century. They chose the area because, according to Monsieur Pinton, who heads the firm of Pinton Freres today, the clear waters of the Creuse were especially suited for dyeing wool. Today the waters remain clear and clean enough for a trout hatchery to flourish right alongside the dyeing works.

Tapestry largely died out as an art form during the 19th century when weavers were concentrating on reproducing paintings rather than designing uniquely for their own medium. This brought them into disrepute in artistic eyes. The realism of 19th century paintings was difficult to capture in woven form. It was the French artist, Jean Lurcat, who revived tapestry in Aubusson in the 1930s by turning towards designs which were considered more suitable for the medium — large expanses of colour and heraldic motifs. Lurcat designed purely for the weavers and encouraged his friends Picasso and Matisse to do the same.

Says John Coburn: 'Tapestry is the ideal decoration for modern architecture. With the vast areas of glass, marble and general starkness, it needs the warmth and richness of tapestry.' He says the sun and the moon come naturally to him in his work — and that they were especially suited as themes for his stylised tapestry curtains.

'I have often used the sun as a religious symbol and it seemed natural to me to use it in the curtains. I wanted to make the Opera Theatre curtain as rich and decorative and theatrical as possible — to give it the rich red and gold quality one associates with opera theatres.'

The richness and boldness of the colouring are indeed suited to the opera theatre. But this very quality is going to pose problems for some set designers — so much so that in some opera productions the Curtain of the Sun will be drawn and replaced by a more sedate neutral curtain during the overture.

For example, in an opera like Fidelio, where much of the action takes place in sombre prison sets, the Curtain of the Sun would contrast too starkly with the mood sought by the set designers. By drawing the bright curtain during the overture the audience will have time to rest their eyes on a neutral colour before the opera begins. The contrast effect will then not be so shattering. Two Sydney theatrical directors have criticised the curtains for this effect: one believes the curtains should hang in a gallery rather than a theatre and the other believes the problem has been solved by the availability of an alternative curtain.

This debate over the effect of the colours on audiences was the second of the curtains' own small, controversies. (It's easy to get the feeling that a part of the Opera House is not really blooded until it's had at least one controversy over it.)

The first controversy came soon after the curtains were first hung — in the rehearsal-recording studio. Pointing out that they had cost $100,000 plus $14,000 import duty, journalists discovered the curtains were showing signs of tearing under their

The abrupt geometry of the wood panelling in the Concert Hall foyer, behind the auditorium's stage.

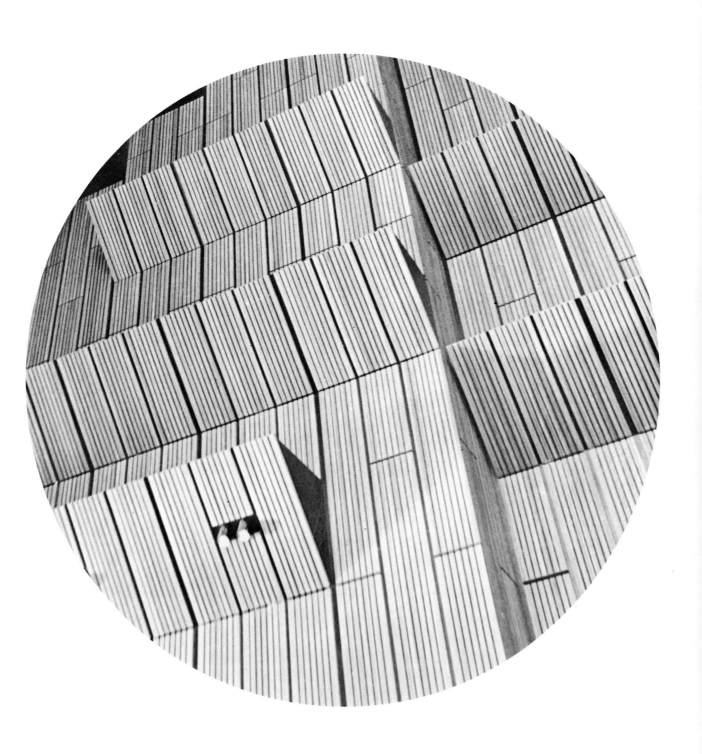

own weight (the Curtain of the Sun weighs 320 lbs and requires six men to carry it).

The enormous weight caused the weaving to stretch where the colours joined and technicians feared the curtains might tear when they were pulled apart for a performance.

Both curtains were taken down and packed away while the Aubusson weavers were consulted on ways of reinforcing them. They advised a special back-stitching to reinforce the weak spots — a project which took three months to complete before the curtains were rehung, with confidence.

Olsen Mural

Night and water,
Pour to one rip of darkness, the Harbour floats,
in air, the Cross hangs upside-down in water.

The Cross refers to Sydney's brightly-lit Kings Cross and the lines above are from the poem Five Bells by the Sydney journalist and man of letters, the late Ken Slessor. They are the inspiration, along with the rest of the poem, for John Olsen's enormous (70 ft by 10 ft) mural, Salute to Slessor's Five Bells, which hangs in the northern foyer of the concert hall.

The $35,000 mural was the first work commissioned by the Sir William Dobell Art Foundation and was its gift to the Opera House. It took nearly a year to complete and illustrates dramatically the words quoted above from the Slessor poem. Its dark purple-blue dominant colour is in rich contrast to the vibrant, bright harbour scene it looks out on in daylight. At night it is part of the harbour, bringing something of the harbour inside the Opera House. It is at its best at night, largely because in daylight the mullions holding the vast glass walls of the foyer reflect on it and interfere with the geometry of its lines.

Olsen painted the mural in a city studio with the assistance of Bob King, a 1930s wrestler who often demolished his opponents with his human torpedo attacks, and Bill Jackson, a coffee shop bouncer from the Depression days, turned picture framer. The two helped him mix paints, brush on extra coats of paint and do the carpentry needed for the massive job. Usually, both are house painters.

The huge, curving mural was moved into place in the Opera House in a two day job in April, 1973. It was divided into eight pieces for the one mile trip from Olsen's studio to Bennelong Point. Later, after it was installed, Olsen resumed work on it to eliminate the joins and make some finishing touches.

But vandals had him at work on the mural much longer than he had planned. He had to repair it after three different attacks: it was spraygunned in black matt paint, in letters three feet high, with an obscene word; scribbled on; and sliced with a nail.

Soon after all these attacks, when security on the painting was intensified, an alert watchman spotted a new attack by graffiti writers. He called a conference

Painter John Olsen supervises assistants at work on his mural.

of security staff who decided that another act of vandalism had been inflicted on the mural and Olsen was called to make the necessary repairs. When he saw the offending mark on the mural, Olsen exploded. It was a part of the painting.

Air Conditioning

You could drive a car through some of the air conditioning duct work in the top area of the highest roof vault of the concert hall — an indication of the enormity of providing a pleasant climate inside this vast and complex building.

Designed by the Danish consulting engineers Steensen and Varming, the $4.5 million plant was installed by Haden Engineering Pty Ltd. It was the biggest air conditioning and fire protection contract ever let in Australia — in keeping with the scale of the whole Opera House project.

There are five miles of steel pipes carrying cool or warm water through the complex. Twenty miles of ductwork distribute air to 3000 outlets and diffusers and 120 fans move more than a million cubic feet of air a minute when the system is working to capacity.

Seawater is pumped from Sydney Harbour into the 1500 ton Frigrite Ltd refrigeration unit in the bowels of the Opera House where it is brought to the required temperature before coursing through the building, stabilising the air temperature and humidity.

In keeping with almost every other aspect of the Opera House construction, the air conditioning presented some unusual problems. One was the need for absolutely silent operation so a lilting aria would not be sung to the accompaniment of a whirring or clanking air duct. Acoustic insulation was used in some ducts, others were built of laminated sheets and every length of ductwork was isolated from the main structure to prevent noise transmission.

The vast glass walls which enclose the northern foyers of both the concert hall and the opera theatre absorb an enormous amount of heat radiation from the sun and greatly increase loading in these areas on the air conditioning system. Other areas have different air conditioning needs.

The stages, for example, have a higher loading on the system caused by the strong lighting which is directed towards them, while the audience areas have a different loading which is affected by the body heat of so many people enclosed in a confined space. To create air conditioning which would meet all the various requirements of the different areas the engineers created several separate but integrated systems.

The drama theatre, for example, has a very low ceiling and the amount of air required to keep its temperature comfortable in such a confined space would blow the audience out of their seats if a normal ducting system was used. A unique system was designed to overcome this problem: an air-cooled aluminium ceiling was installed to supplement the normal blower system and to cool the ceiling lights.

In the concert hall, many of the outlets have been designed as a part of the décor — in the form of cannon-like projections from the walls where they have a patterned effect. Other outlets are placed around the ceiling lights. Some of the conditioned air is removed through the spotlights to cool them.

A Honeywell computer manned by a single operator controls the whole integrated system. The operator can dial the temperature for any area in the whole Opera House complex. At the same time he can identify any alarms — such as a dirty filter which needs replacing or a breakdown which needs urgent attention — from numbers which are flashed on to the screen of a scanner. A permanent record of alarms is kept on computer printout which gives engineers an opportunity to check the long term operating efficiency of various parts of the system.

Auxiliary Power

The Opera House has its own emergency power system which will cut in automatically in the event of a power failure. The system supplies power for aisle lights, direction signs and escape lights in stairs, corridors, plant rooms, main dressing rooms and other areas. It is a battery based system and emergency power will come from a 12-ton nickel cadmium alkaline battery. It incorporates twin 240-volt batteries which combined are able to carry an emergency load of 95 kilowatts for two hours. These consist of 380 cells which are assembled in two parallel banks and their total capacity is 110 ampere hours.

Seating

The seats in all auditoria are of the same design, though they are covered with a variety of colours. They are built of white birch plywood which gives solidity and bass retention — an acoustic consideration. Each chair cost $200 including installation. They have aluminium pedestals and framework. Polyurethane provides the padding which was designed so that it would be hard enough to keep people awake but soft enough to be comfortable during a long performance. A specially designed hydraulic plunger makes them return slowly to their upright position, thus making them noiseless. Ergonomic mannequins were used to test the chairs before their final shape was developed.

Fire Protection

There are more than 8000 fire protection sprinklers in the Opera House. Sprinkler heads have been installed in the ceilings of the two main auditoria to protect the seating and furnishing below and a further system of sprinklers has been installed in the voids between the ceilings and the roof shells to protect the ceilings themselves. Further protection is provided by special automatic gas systems which will put out a fire without water damage to the expensive electronic equipment.

Concert Organ

Ronald Sharp, an Australian, has designed and is building the massive organ which is partly installed in the concert hall. It is scheduled for completion in 1976 and will be the largest mechanical organ in the world with 127 stops and comprising 10,500 pipes. More than 100 pipes, in burnished tin, and 24 bronze bells, give the instrument its completed appearance in the concert hall, above the platform.

Room Service

Star performers and key staff at the Opera House have at their fingertips a luxury hotel style piece of electronic gadgetry that makes them feel thoroughly pampered (something essential for many of the world's top artists using the theatre complex).

This gadget is in itself the star performer of the Opera House's amazing web of electronics that is probably the most advanced installed in any performing arts centre anywhere in the world. It is a room service module installed in star artists' dressing rooms and in the offices of top staff.

For example, it permits a symphony orchestra conductor to tune an instrument in his dressing room without the aid of a tuning fork. Through his room service module he can call up the precise sound he needs, with all the overtones produced by an oboe, the instrument used most frequently for tuning.

The same conductor may call up the stage manager by pressing a button on the module and, speaking from anywhere in his suite in a normal conversational tone, his voice is relayed to the stage manager's desk. The system works both ways, if the stage manager wants to speak with the conductor.

Closed circuit television on the module gives the conductor a chance to get an early look at the audience, or watch his orchestra tuning up or rehearsing. He may even look at another performance in another auditorium in the Opera House. Later, after his performance, he can, if he wants, relax in his dressing room and watch a movie on the module. The same module provides him with a telephone which allows him to call the world or order a meal from the catering service. Less sophisticated systems are installed in all other dressing rooms and in many other staff offices.

Translation System

Because the Opera House — especially the concert hall — is a venue for international conventions, the planners have installed a translation system similar to that used in the United Nations.

During such international conferences and conventions the speaker's words are picked up by a microphone and transmitted to a sound-proof booth where a translator instantly converts the speech into another language. Translations pass back to the audience by radio earphones. The system is capable of handling five different languages and, in addition to the concert hall, it serves the opera theatre. Three language translations are available in the drama theatre, the chamber music hall-cinema and the recital room.

Lighting

So vast was the job of lighting the Opera House that two of Australia's biggest lighting companies, GEC and Philips, united to form a special consortium — GEC-Philips Opera House Lighting Co. Pty Ltd. The complexity of the task drew on all the local and overseas resources and expertise of the joint company, both in design and manufacturing.

British and Dutch lighting consultants from the two partners were briefed so that a comprehensive lighting philosophy and plan could be drawn up — with a primary objective of highlighting the building's unique architecture. But, at the same time, the lighting had to be functional.

Externally, the problem was to highlight the soaring white shells against the blackness of the harbour at night, without either interrupting the shipping signals of the Maritime Services Board or irritating the Opera House's residential neighbours in their home units and flats across the narrow channel of water in Kirribilli.

The solution to contrasting the Opera House against the harbour was relatively simple: the building's unique form with its many sympathetic shapes, the whiteness of the shells' surfaces and the shadow created by each shell on its neighbour called for floodlighting. But it had to be precisely positioned to eliminate problems with the Maritime Services Board and the residents of Kirribilli. Critical analysis of the location of each tungsten halogen lamp and accurate direction of its flood of light has successfully overcome the problems posed by the highly reflective nature of the shells.

The solution has eliminated all possible irritations and left the Opera House at night illuminated by a flood of white light reminiscent of some latter day Indian temple bathed in bright moonlight.

Inside, the problems were similar, though more intricate. There was a wealth of contrasting shapes and forms which would create their own special patterns of light and shade to highlight the visual impact of the structure. While there was no problem of annoying neighbours or interrupting shipping signals there was the problem of making the lighting functional to suit the special needs of each separate area of the building without offending the integrity of the architecture.

For example, the high ceilings of both the concert hall and the opera theatre have enabled effective use of high intensity incandescent down lights. But from

Seats and boxes, Opera Theatre.

there onwards the lighting design had to cope with the special needs of the two halls.

In the concert hall where activities would be largely concerned with listening, rather than watching and listening, the decor is light and bright with considerable visual impact. Incandescent directional lighting has been used extensively here to highlight this impact.

But in the opera theatre, where the audience attention needs riveting to the stage, the decor is softer and darker so there is no visual interference with the activity on the stage. The lighting here is softer, to fit the decor, and directional lighting is aimed only at the stage.

In the drama theatre and the music room, much smaller areas to light than the concert hall and opera theatre, fluorescent lighting is used, with provision for dimming. In all the performing areas glare is virtually non-existent.

The overall lighting design was developed with the use of a scale model of the Opera House complex which was built by the GEC-Philips engineers. Scaled lighting installed in the model enabled them to calculate precisely the effects of all lighting on the design of the two main halls.

Some specialised lamps were built by the British and Dutch principal companies of the consortium partners but almost all the lighting equipment, particularly the fittings, were made in Australia.

The Stage that Never Was

When on March 21, 1967, the NSW Cabinet adopted the alternative plan for the Opera House which meant changing the major auditorium from a dual purpose concert-opera hall to a single purpose concert hall and changing the minor auditorium from a drama theatre to the opera theatre, a great deal of work had to be undone.

Among other things, the stage in the big hall was concreted over for acoustical reasons. But one of the big wastes was the proscenium arch and stage tower machinery, which had been already partly installed. The machinery was ordered from the Austrian firm of Wagner-Biro in 1961 at a reported cost of $3.5 million, when the 'final' cost of the Opera House was estimated at a mere $10 million.

Today, what is left of the machinery is wasting away in a paddock next door to a government penal institution. Some of it is lying exposed to the weather beneath the tattered remains of tarpaulins and some of it in the crates in which it was shipped to Australia. Soon after it was scrapped authorities said much of the machinery would be used in the redesigned opera theatre but this proved impossible and it was left to rot.

The Opera House Trust

The Sydney Opera House Trust, which was formed, somewhat ahead of time, in 1961 is responsible for the running of the Opera House as a going concern.

Vermillion seats and blue carpet in the Drama Theatre.

The structure for the revolving stage that never was.

It is headed by Sir Philip Baxter, the distinguished nuclear scientist, who is chairman. Other members are Lady Macarthur-Onslow, Mr S. F. Buckley, Mr Justice Jacobs, Sir Asher Joel, Sir Robert Norman, Mr A. H. Urquhart, Mr H. L. Yelland, Mr C. G. Meckiff (director of the State Ministry of Cultural Activities), and Mr P. E. Taylor.

The manager of the Opera House, Mr Frank Barnes, is responsible to the Trust. The permanent labour force at the Opera House includes 75 in the technical manager's department, 75 in the service manager's department, about 40 in the box offices and 45 in administration, 60 in house management which includes security and about 15 in publicity. Casual staff varies between 150 and 200.

Having cost $100 million the Opera House probably will never make a profit. It will probably continue to operate on a subsidy from the State Government of $1 for every $1 it earns. It will cost about $3½ million a year to operate and in its first year of operation the NSW Government allowed for a subsidy of $1.5 million. The annual wages bill — the biggest component — amounts to about $1.5 million. Power and lighting costs are estimated at an annual $300,000 and cleaning costs are about the same. Maintenance for elevators, stage machinery and lighting will account for about $150,000 annually. As the building ages, maintenance costs will rise.

About half the money to meet running costs will come from rents and the concessions for food and drink. But the Trust will supplement this to a small degree by becoming an entrepreneur itself. It will engage performers itself. But most of its money will come from rents: $750 a night plus six per cent of ticket revenue for the Concert Hall; $5200 a week plus six per cent of ticket sales for the Opera Theatre. The drama theatre costs $1000 a week plus six per cent. In each case the hirer gets full use of all facilities and free access to rehearsal rooms.

The Stars

Everybody in Sydney has had something to say about the Opera House. So why not an astrologer, Dennis Oakland, who points out that the building will have teething troubles but its ruling planet, Venus, will counter-balance these.

He told a newspaper: 'Venus will endow the Opera House with strong imagination and a temperament that is drawn to beauty, possessions and luxury.'

For its first year, he made the following predictions for the Opera House:
November 7, 1973: Possible introduction of a great new work. Peace and agreement between staff and management.
November 29: New agreements on financial matters, government sponsorship and salary awards.
December 18: Could be a brilliant but somewhat disruptive day.
January 9 and 10, 1974: Financial difficulties through lack of budget discipline.

January 30: Staff demanding more money.
March 10 and 11: A continuation of the above problems. Staff problems and arguments and internal strife and lack of initiative in decisions.
May 2: A financial windfall which could settle the previous problems.
August 4: Possible crisis in financial and union affairs.
August 17: Time of opportunity for excellent new productions.
December 30: Much energy and financial resources should improve.
February 21, 1975: New gains in popularity. General increases in attendances at performances.

In Brief

The Opera House covers four and a half acres.

It contains more than 900 rooms.

The podium reaches a maximum height of 50 feet.

At the landward end it is 312 feet wide and almost all of its width comprises the enormous open air staircase.

From the first step to the Harbour's edge at the back of the building is 600 feet.

The highest roof shell is 221 feet above sea level.

The roofs comprise 2194 prefabricated concrete sections weighing up to 15 tons each and held together by epoxy glue and 217 miles of tensioned steel cable.

There are 1,056,000 tiles attached to 4240 concrete 'lids' covering the shells.

The podium contains 125,000 tons of concrete and 6,000 tons of steel.

The roof system weighes 26,800 tons and is supported on 550 concrete piers three feet in diameter and 32 columns from four to eight feet square.

The concert hall roof is 400 feet long and 176 feet wide.

The Opera Theatre is 174 feet high, 352 feet long and 128 feet wide.

There is 67,000 square feet of topaz-tinted, laminated glass three-quarters of an inch thick.

The costs rose this way year by year:
1957, $7 million; 1958, $10 million;
1961, $17 million; 1962, $24 million;
1964, $34 million; 1965, $48 million;
1968, $85 million; 1972, $99 million;
1973, $100 million.

The
Troubled
Triumphant
Story

Sydney in the 1950s was a bustling place. Like the rest of Australia, only more so, it was enjoying the Korean War boom and it was sharing the nation's highest-ever ride on the sheep's back. Wool was fetching unheard-of prices and property values were soaring. They were expansive times. The city's population was edging up towards the two million mark. Expanding with the population, which was receiving a massive fillip from post-war European migration, was Sydney's cultural soul.

Sydney had always been a city of lovers of symphony concerts and European immigrants were boosting the numbers of concert goers. Eugene Goossens, who had taken up the joint post of director of the New South Wales Conservatorium and conductor of the Sydney Symphony Orchestra in 1947, was an enthusiastic promoter of music. He was determined to mould the SSO into a first-rate group and he was succeeding. His promotion of the orchestra was rubbing off on Sydney. The city was taking more and more pride in its orchestra and its people were patronising performances as they had never done before.

Performances were held in the Sydney Town Hall, a massive chunk of High Victorian wedding cake architecture which was the only suitable venue in Sydney for large-audience live shows. It served the city in a multitude of roles from public meetings to SSO concerts. But its acoustics were poor. Goossens wanted a better home for his orchestra. And he had no hesitation in pushing for it.

There had been talk for many years before of a cultural centre or an opera house or an arts complex in Sydney. But the atmosphere then, in the late 1940s and early 1950s, was as receptive as it had ever been. The city was beginning to think, in those heady days, that it could afford to treat itself to something grand in the way of a home for the performing arts.

As early as 1947, Goossens was actively campaigning for an opera house and though he was to change his mind several times on where it should be built his first choice was always Bennelong Point.

There were supporters for the proposal to build an opera house, though there was little agreement on just where. On October 6, 1948 Goossens told a Sydney audience that the idea of building an opera house on Bennelong Point had originally been raised with a city planner in discussions on cultural centres which should be included in a master plan for Sydney. At the time Bennelong Point was occupied by a tram shed. Goossens told his audience:

'Many considerations are entailed besides the important one of alternative accommodation for Sydney's trams, but I am confident of winning the interest and sympathetic co-operation of the government in this regard. Only the prize-winning architectural design of an international competition (which I hope an Australian wins) will be worthy of such a site. Like the San Francisco War Memorial Opera House, it must furnish a permanent home for our symphony orchestra, opera, ballet and choral

festivals. The auditorium must accommodate audiences of from 3500 to 4000 — no fewer.'

The following day the then Minister for Local Government, Mr J. J. (Joe) Cahill (he was later to become the Premier who gave reality to the dreams of an opera house) said the master plan for Sydney made no provision for an opera house on Bennelong Point but that it did provide for cultural centres to be built. The then acting Premier, Mr J. M. Baddeley, said he was interested in Goossens' proposal. The Transport Minister of the day added that he favoured the building of an opera house for Sydney but he didn't want to lose the tram sheds on Bennelong Point. A few days later Goossens was at it again. On October 20, 1948 he was predicting that Sydney would have an opera house on Bennelong Point.

'We must have the opera house within five years,' he said.

'Sydney orchestra is taking its place among the world's major symphonic groups. A fine hall is essential if the public is to hear the orchestra at its best. If my plan succeeds Sydney will have, with the co-operation of those in authority, a great opera house. There is substantial support for the site and we intend to follow it up.'

The proposal to build an opera house was taking root in the minds of Sydney's influential people of the time. So was the proposal to build it on Bennelong Point. It had certainly taken root in the mind of J. J. Cahill.

Cahill became Premier of New South Wales in 1952, the culmination of a long, self-made political career. He was Sydney-born (1891) of Irish Catholic working class parents and began working as an apprentice fitter and turner at age 15. But he continued his education at night school, became active in union activities and eventually entered the State Parliament in 1925 where he spent 16 years as a back bencher before becoming a Minister (for Works) at age 50. When Cahill became Premier in 1952 Goossens and his supporters were still enthusiastically pushing their idea of an opera house on Bennelong Point. Their campaign was gaining momentum. The Sydney newspapers' correspondence columns were frequently filled with debate on the sort of opera house or cultural centre the city needed. And sites for such a building were argued back and forth.

The discussion came to a head early in 1954 when Goossens returned from a trip to Europe and proposed a plan to build an opera house close to the central business district, near the Wynyard railway station. (He said he had long relinquished his vision of Bennelong Point and was resigned to it remaining a tram shed in the clutches of the then Transport Minister.) This revitalised the opera house proposals. The city had virtually accepted the idea that Sydney was going to have an opera house and now all that needed to be settled was the site. The State government, however, had made no decision.

But Cahill recognised that Sydney had convinced itself that an opera house was going to be built. His own taste in entertainment tended more towards watching horse racing than an evening at a symphony concert and he apparently had no desire to establish himself as a premier who was a great patron of the arts. He may have wanted to leave a lasting monument to his years as premier and to his government but he already had been responsible for establishing a State dockyard and State brick manufacturing concern. These were achievements for which he would probably have preferred to be remembered.

Nevertheless the opera house idea appealed to him and to galvanise all the discussion into action would have been a feather in the black homburg hat he wore. Once he had begun his project the people of New South Wales were to see more of the Cahill determination, the sort that had brought him from the slums of Redfern to the highest office in the State. Once he had taken to the idea he pushed it ahead with such verve and vigour that it can now be generally conceded that Cahill alone forced the construction of the Opera House that now stands on Bennelong Point.

He had mentioned it many times but on November 8, 1954, Cahill formally announced that the State government would build an opera house and that a meeting would be convened to discuss sites, designs and uses of the building. A week earlier Cahill and the then Lord Mayor of Sydney, Pat Hills (later to become leader of the State Opposition), had agreed that selection of a site was an urgent matter. They had also agreed on some sharing of costs and that a conference of interested parties should be convened to get the project moving.

Cahill called a meeting in Sydney's Public Library on November 30, 1954 — 'a conference of persons and organisations interested in the establishment of an Opera House in Sydney,' said the Sydney Morning Herald in its report of the meeting the next day.

The paper went on: 'The conference unanimously supported the establishment of an Opera House in Sydney and agreed to set up a committee to investigate suggestions for its site and design.'

The committee selected was: Eugene Goossens; Professor Henry Ingham Ashworth, dean of the Faculty of Architecture at Sydney University; Charles (later Sir Charles) Moses, general manager of the Australian Broadcasting Commission (which administers and largely finances the symphony orchestras of the six State capitals of Australia); Roy G. Hendy, the Town Clerk of Sydney, and Mr Stanley Haviland, the under-secretary of the Department of Local Government.

Cahill said the government had no preconceived ideas about the site or design of the proposed Opera House (this was about when the misnomer was tagged to the project) but it thought the building should be a monument worthy of Sydney. Remember that at this time Sydney was flexing itself, keen to be a major city and they were times of boom. A monument worthy of Sydney in this context would, indeed, have to be monumental.

'Sydney's Opera House,' said Cahill, 'will be the first in Australia and it is probably many years since a similar project was undertaken anywhere in the world. This country just cannot go on without proper facilities for the expression of talent and the staging of the highest forms of artistic entertainment. I appeal to all those persons and organisations interested in the project to be big in every way about it and if a site is chosen which perhaps does not satisfy all their views, they should continue to give their wholehearted support . . . The opportunities for erecting monumental buildings in Sydney are rare and I agree that while we must be practical, the Opera House must be something that the people of this city and the State can be proud of.'

Cahill said that the purpose of the conference was to enable the government to hear the views of as many groups as possible, to draw on the experience of people who were interested in opera, drama and ballet and who might possibly have investigated or been associated with opera both in Australia and overseas.

Goossens followed Cahill with an outline of the points which the committee would have to consider. These were the purposes to which the building was to be devoted; the size and nature of a structure required to meet these purposes; the site considered most suitable and the constitution of a permanent board of management. Goossens again plumped for his first choice for a site: Bennelong Point, though he conceded there were other sites to be considered. But he felt compelled to say that Bennelong Point offered plenty of space and that on this site the Opera House would be visible to ships entering the Harbour and Sydney people could proudly point out their Opera House to visitors.

Mr Cahill envisaged spending about £1 million to £1.5 million ($3 million) on the project.

The Momentum Grows

While Cahill had mentioned a figure between £1 million and £1.5 million as a total cost of the Opera House, no firm directive on costs was given to the committee (Stanley Haviland was elected its chairman) chosen that November 30, 1954. The committee therefore decided to ignore such considerations and pressed ahead with what it saw as its prime functions. A site had to be selected, the requirements of the building had to be decided and a design selected. While the public tried to help — filling column after column of the opinion pages of the Sydney newspapers, the committee worked on.

It approached the Royal Australian Institute of Architects to advise on the selection of a site. The institute appointed a special committee to investigate — though investigation appears to have been rather a formality since the various possible sites had been exhaustively canvassed in the years before. This committee was Professor Ashworth, Mr Walter Bunning, a distinguished Sydney architect, and

Professor Denis Winston, who was Professor of Town and Country Planning at Sydney University. They recommended Bennelong Point.

On May 17, 1955 the NSW Cabinet announced that it had decided to adopt Bennelong Point as the site for the Opera House. The tram depot would be relinquished by the State Transport Department as it phased out trams and introduced buses in the city. Fort Macquarie, as the tram shed was called, would be demolished to make way for the Opera House. At the same time as it accepted the committee's advice on a site, the government also agreed with its suggestion that the Opera House should contain two main halls — one seating 3500 people and the other seating 1200. The larger hall, the committee said, would be used for ballet, orchestral and choral performances as well as for opera. The smaller hall, it said, was the only proper solution for intimate theatre.

In considering the site, the committee had agreed that the Opera House should be within the city boundaries, close to the traffic network, but not on a main artery, and providing adequate parking facilities. The committee said it had considered 21 sites and after rejecting a number of these it had reviewed the other suggestions in the light of these requirements: the building had to be so located that it would neither dominate nor be dominated by other buildings; the site had to be in a setting where full rein could be given to architectural expression; the project had to be capable of being completed within a reasonable time.

'Consideration of these factors led the committee to the unanimous conclusion that Bennelong Point is the outstanding suitable site,' the committee's report stated. 'With the removal of the tram depot, sufficient area will be available for the building, its approach roads, surrounding garden area and parking space for about 200 cars. More ample parking space will be available nearby during the evening periods when it will be required. It can be conveniently served by bus, train, tram and ferry transport. Above all, the site being on a predominant headland of Sydney's magnificent waterway will provide a setting unique in the world for a building of such monumental character as an Opera House.'

Goossens had won. Sydney applauded. *The Sydney Morning Herald*, in an editorial the following day, reflected the community reaction to the government's decision.

'By its choice of Bennelong Point as the site for Sydney's Opera House, State Cabinet performed an act of rare imagination,' it said. 'No finer site for a great theatre exists in the world, and if the government and people of New South Wales now show the same determination in building it they will do much to make amends for the long years of neglect of our waterfront. It is of course one thing to choose a beautiful site and another to build a beautiful theatre. There is a great deal still to be decided. How it is to be financed. How much of the total the State Government is prepared to pay.

Professor H. Ingham Ashworth.

Whether the design will be thrown open to international competition or restricted to Australian architects and — almost more important — who are to be the judges. (These at least should be international.) The actual form of the building also presents serious problems. The committee is almost certainly wise in recommending that two theatres should be built under the same roof. But something will presumably depend on an estimate of the cost, and this would be an expensive project. The important thing now is to make these decisions as quickly as possible. Mr Cahill deserves credit for his energy in a matter where he may think that there are few votes to be gained and possibly some to be lost; but Sydneysiders will remember him with gratitude if in a few years time they can share with the citizens of Stockholm and Venice the civilised pleasure of hearing great music in a perfect setting beside the waters of their own matchless harbour.'

It was an interesting editorial. In fact the committee had foreshadowed some of the *Herald's* suggestions. It had, for example, said that the next step was to decide on a design and that, probably, a competition would be held. The committee estimated that it would take about a year to organise a competition and at least another year to produce working drawings from the winning design. But the *Herald's* editorial itself foreshadowed some of the problems that were to haunt the Opera House through its stormy history — and nobody had an idea of what it was going to look like.

There was a great deal of public debate over whether an international competition should be held to find a design for the Opera House — indeed whether there should be a competition at all. Certainly, Cahill favoured an approach to a selected, first-rate Australian architect who would submit sketches and, finally, be commissioned to design the building. This plan was also favoured by Walter Bunning, one of the architects who had worked on the panel which selected Bennelong Point as the site. The reasons against an international competition varied from the difficulties of organising it, to the cost involved, to pure nationalism which demanded the commissioning of an Australian architect. But the arguments for the international competition were persuasive, especially in the context of the chosen site and the philosophy behind that choice. The building had to be the best opera house that Sydney could build. If Sydney wanted the best possible brains behind the design it had to hold a competition and it had to be an international one.

The executive committee charged with guiding the Opera House concept towards its birth was quickly convinced of this and settled down to its chief problem — would the competition result in the best possible design? It is recognised by architects that in competitions of this nature the judges are almost as important as the entrants. A panel had to be chosen before the competition could be announced. Possible judges were sounded out; they had to be distinguished architects so that they would have the

Bennelong, after whom the site was named.
(From a Lithograph in the Mitchell Library).

Old Fort Macquarie tramsheds.

confidence of their professional colleagues who entered the competition. And international architects' professional bodies had to be consulted on conditions for the competition and their approval sought so that their members could enter.

It was four months of solid work before the State Government announced, on September 13, 1955, that it would hold a competition for the design. First prize was to be £5000 ($10,000); second prize £2000 ($4000) and third prize £1000 ($2000). Four assessors would be appointed; two from Australia and one each from the United States and Britain. One of the two Australians was to be Professor Ashworth, who had been so close to the project since its earliest stages. He was to be chairman of the panel. He was Manchester born but had come to Australia in 1949 and had become Dean of the Faculty of Architecture at Sydney University. The other Australian assessor (judge to the layman) was to be Cobden Parkes, then the New South Wales' Government Architect and a son of one of the founders of Australian Federation, Sir Henry Parkes. The two foreign assessors were yet to be named.

They were found and named on November 7. Eero Saarinen, who had designed the acclaimed General Motors Technical Centre in Detroit and the TWA Terminal at Kennedy International Airport, New York, and who had won competitions for his designs of theatres and concert halls, was to be the American representative. Dr John Leslie Martin, who had designed London's Royal Festival Hall (much admired by Goossens) and who was Professor of Architecture at Cambridge University, was to be the British representative.

Closing time for the competition was set at 5 pm on December 3, 1956. (This was later extended to take in entries which had been postmarked before that time.)

By January 1956 the executive committee and the government had agreed on what they wanted inside the edifice that was to be built on Bennelong Point. The scheme was that architects who wanted to enter were to pay a £10 ($20) registration fee for which they would receive the complete details, including pictures of the site, the building regulations in the city of Sydney, what precisely was wanted and the conditions of entry. A 25-page booklet was published containing all this information. It called for the design of 'a national opera house' which would consist of two halls, one seating 3000 to 3500 people and the other for about 1200 people. There also had to be a restaurant with seating for 250 people, two meeting rooms (one for 200 people and the other for 100), rehearsal rooms, offices, and facilities for film and broadcasting.

The main hall had to be designed for 'symphony concerts (including organ music) and soloists, large scale opera, ballet and dance, choral, pageants and mass meetings.' The smaller hall had to fulfil these functions: 'Dramatic presentations, intimate opera, chamber music, concerts and recitals, lectures.' This was the order in which the functions of the Opera

House were set down by the government. They were to become objects of great argument later. The winner of the competition was to be engaged by the government to build the opera house.

Most people were pleased with the government announcement of the competition and publication of the conditions in a booklet was at last something tangible after nearly 10 years of talk.

The people who showed their displeasure most at the whole project were the tramwaymen who were going to lose their tramshed on Bennelong Point. They went on strike in protest against the demolition of the ersatz fortress, Fort Macquarie, which surrounded the tram depot.

The world's architects had almost a year to produce their designs. When the government finally closed entries in December, 1956, it had received 233 designs. Australians submitted 61, Britons 53, West Germans 26, Americans 24. More than 700 architects had registered and almost 500 forfeited their fee after they had seen the conditions of the competition.

Professor Martin flew into Sydney on January 7, 1957 and Saarinen followed him four days later. Immediately Saarinen arrived he was taken to lunch and then to Bennelong Point, where he became entranced by its possibilities as a site for the Opera House. The four judges were at work within hours of Saarinen's arrival. They had been allocated a large room in the Art Gallery of New South Wales. There were no pictures hanging in the room and there was plenty of wall space for the judges to hang drawings from the various designs to help in their assessments.

Some of the entries contained as many as 30 drawings (working drawings were not required). Postage on some of them ran as high as $80 and, while the government had insured each entry for $800, the judges thought some of the designs represented $3000 worth of work. Designs submitted were numbered and coded so that the identity of the architect was known only to the chairman of the opera house executive committee, Stanley Haviland.

On January 18 the judges handed their selections (they had to choose first, second and third prizes) and a report on them to Haviland at an informal ceremony in the Lands Department building, one of a series of buildings comprising a cityscape which the National Trust classifies as a highly important piece of Victorian architecture.

The judges had worked quickly and solidly.

'It was almost a night and day job,' said Saarinen, 'except for a Sunday morning we took off to go to Palm Beach. But a most pleasant job to work on.'

The effusive Saarinen (who also stammered) added: 'The judging has been most cordial. And you can say that our choices were unanimous. Absolutely unanimous.'

Indeed, they had been unanimous, but they had also been a victory for Saarinen himself. The winning design had been already marked down to go on the short list when Saarinen arrived (late) for the judging.

When he saw Joern Utzon's drawings — having seen the site only hours before — he was wildly enthusiastic. It was an extraordinary and complex proposal and the other judges had their reservations. But to every objection they made Saarinen had an answer. He convinced them, though it's hard to believe that their objections to the design were terribly strong. They WERE looking for a monumental building.

The Winning Design

'A piece of Danish pastry,' one critic called it. Another said, 'It looks like an insect with a shell on its back which has just crawled out from under a log.'

But most called it magnificent, imaginative, a piece of poetry, outstanding art, and monumental.

At least the views were strong. Nobody was disappointed — except for the secretary of the State Parks and Playgrounds Movement, who said, 'The design would occupy the whole of the site at Bennelong Point. We were given to understand that the small reserve at present existing would be preserved. We are very disappointed.'

What they were talking about was a piece of extraordinary architectural design, something so imaginative and yet so simple in concept, something that made architects' jaws drop and something that boggled the minds of structural engineers. It was, in essence, a massive chunk of rock covered by billowing white-tile vaults that appeared to be sails. It would look as though Bennelong Point itself was under full sail and cruising out into the harbour from the city.

What they were talking about was the design that had come from the fertile mind of a 38-year-old Dane, named Joern Utzon. Joern who? The world was soon to know.

It had been with more than a little sense of occasion that Premier Cahill invited an audience to hear him announce the result of the international competition in the NSW Art Gallery on the afternoon of January 29, 1957. Cahill knew the importance of his announcement; it was the culmination of 10 years of talk and very little action; and it meant much to him as Premier and to his government, especially in the eyes of the New South Wales voters. He pushed the suspense inherent in the occasion to its limit. He kept stalling — almost half an hour. And with Hitchcock-like timing he slowly tore open the envelope at 3.29 pm and read the results — a series of numbers that were meaningless to the audience. 'I'm afraid I haven't got the names of the winners,' he teased.

The key to the number coding was quickly produced and the Premier announced that the competition had been won by Joern Utzon, aged 38, of Helleback, Denmark. Second place had gone to a Philadelphia group, J. Marzella, L. Loschetter, W. Cunningham, W. Weissman, N. Brecher, R. Geddes

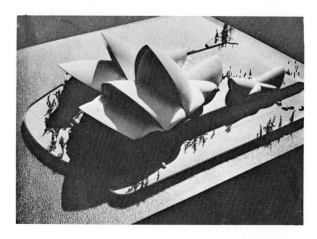

A model of Utzon's original concept: softer in its curves and perhaps more graceful than the finished product, but impossible to build.

and G. Qualls. Third prize was won by a British firm, Boissevain and Osmond.

Sketches accompanying Utzon's entry — and one that had been specially prepared in colour at Sydney University, for Utzon had omitted a perspective of his vision — revealed what the Dane had in mind for Bennelong Point. And as the soaring sail-like design became slowly more clear, especially to architects, it was seen that in his visually astounding building Utzon had made both the extreme beauty and the extreme difficulties of the site work together to achieve a most functional structure. In his clean break with convention, visually and structurally, he had created a monument that also solved many of the design problems the project presented.

The storm clouds were mere droplets of condensation, high in the air and far away. Happiness, on that summer afternoon in Sydney, was Utzon's Opera House on Bennelong Point.

The Site

Utzon had not seen Sydney Harbour or Bennelong Point when he drew his winning sketches of an opera house. He had seen only photographs of the site — hundreds of them, he said. And yet his soaring sails capture the very spirit of Sydney Harbour like no other building along the foreshore. His monument on Bennelong Point is right. For it is here, or a little to the west in Sydney Cove, the tiny pocket of water that is Circular Quay, that the Australian nation was founded.

Dutch and Portuguese explorers had sailed Australian waters extensively — even circumnavigated the continent — more than 100 years before James Cook. But it was Lieutenant Cook who claimed the eastern coast of the continent for Great Britain, in 1770, after sailing from Point Hicks in the south to Cape York in the north. On his way up the coast he had stopped in at and named Botany Bay, for its profusion of flora, but he bypassed what was to become Sydney Harbour, merely noting that inside the two great rocky headlands there appeared to be a good deep water port, which he named Port Jackson, after George Jackson, Advocate General of the British Fleet. Some time after Cook had reported on this voyage to the Admiralty, the British Government was casting around for a likely piece of land to establish a penal colony, to relieve the inhuman crowding of its domestic prisons. The east coast of Australia, specifically Botany Bay, was chosen. And a junior naval officer, Lieutenant Arthur Phillip, who had retired to become a farmer, was chosen to lead the expedition, with a promotion to captain.

He left Portsmouth on May 13, 1787, in command of 11 ships carrying about 800 convicts, 250 marines, 200 merchant sailors and 200 Royal Navy officers and ratings. The fleet reached Botany Bay on January 18, 1788 but Phillip was disappointed with the place. It was too flat and there was no shelter from the winds. And there was no water.

A sketch accompanying Utzon's entry in the design competition.

A sketch of Utzon's original concept. It staggered the engineers and made Sydney gasp when unveiled as the competition winner.

Phillip mounted a small expedition to sail northwards up the coast to look at this Port Jackson that Cook had mentioned as being a good deep water port. Inside the headlands, North Head and South Head as they are unimaginatively known today, Phillip knew that this was the harbour he needed to shelter his fleet and his unfortunate charges. About four miles into the harbour from where he first landed just inside the heads Phillip found what he wanted. A small, well-sheltered cove with a small stream of fresh water running into it. It was also fairly well hidden from view from the heads and out of cannon range from there — two important considerations since England was almost always at war.

On January 25 he anchored his fleet on Sydney Cove. The following day a ground party went ashore under Phillip's command to raise the English flag and name the new colony Sydney, after Viscount Sydney, then secretary of the Home Department and administrator of colonial affairs. Phillip also gave the name of Sydney to his little cove.

It is now generally agreed that the flag raising ceremony took place on a spot somewhere near the monolithic yellow sandstone building which houses the Maritime Services Board at Circular Quay, and a small plaque marks this spot today.

When Phillip arrived in Sydney Cove the eastern tip of the point, which was to be named later as Bennelong Point, was in fact a small island separated from the mainland by a narrow and shallow channel. Because of this Phillip found it ideal as a place to keep his livestock. They were unloaded here and the place became known as Cattle Point. Phillip and his military men and convicts did not, of course, have the glorious shores of Sydney Harbour to themselves. There were local Aboriginal tribes, some of whom were quite friendly, others a little stand-offish and some quite hostile to the white settlers. Phillip thought it a good idea to maintain friendly contact with them and in 1789 he appointed Australia's first public relations man — Bennelong, a young, well built and apparently courageous Aboriginal named Bennelong. Bennelong learned some English and became an interpreter and pivot between the white and black communities around Sydney Cove. Phillip liked him immensely and kept him well supplied with the alcohol Bennelong drank with relish. Bennelong later entertained the new settlers with his intoxicated swaggering as he mimicked Phillip's French chef. A small hut was built for him on the point, which took his name.

Governor Phillip was recalled in 1792. His superiors in Britain were well pleased with the way in which he had established the colony and especially the way in which he had brought it — despite some very serious times when the residents went close to starving — almost to self-sufficiency. Phillip took Bennelong with him when he left Sydney Cove, along with another Aboriginal named Yemmerrawannie. Yemmerrawannie died in England but Bennelong was a smash hit with society and was fascinated by

Captain Arthur Phillip lands at Sydney Cove.

The delicate louvre structure.

his importance. When he returned to Australia three years later he was more self-important, more swaggering than ever. And he drank more liquor. But eventually he disappeared into the bush, went 'walkabout' and historical consensus says he was killed in a tribal war in 1813.

By 1817 the military based in Sydney had seen the need to fortify their tiny outpost in the Southern Hemisphere, because of Britain's constant state of belligerence, and a small fortress was built on Bennelong Point to defend against any intruders who came too far up the harbour. (The small channel of water was filled in.) Later a complete fort was built, heavily armed and manned against what was then considered to be the real threat of a Russian, French or American invasion. This large square fort, built of locally quarried sandstone, was called Fort Macquarie after the governor who had administered the colony between 1810 and 1821. Under Macquarie, convicts released were encouraged to take up land and become productive, John Macarthur's development of a local wool industry from Merino sheep was helped along and the colony began to evolve an architectural style in the many public buildings that were erected. Despite his arrogance which grew almost intolerable in the last years of his administration, Macquarie was regarded as a most progressive Governor who helped the colony to grow as fast as possible.

In 1902 the troops were moved out of Fort Macquarie, its armaments were removed and the building demolished. In its place the government of the day erected a tram shed. But no ordinary tram shed. As if to apologise for putting such a building on such a site they decided that it should at least be an imposing tram shed. The building was given turrets and mock battlements. Inside, nothing but trams. On this historic site stood the tram shed and a small park until demolition began in 1959 to make way for the Sydney Opera House.

Accept the tram shed as a travesty of historical justice to this site, which does command a high place in the Australian story. It is fitting that a public building of the stature of the Opera House should stand there today. Bennelong Point deserves it. That is the historical view.

From an aesthetic point of view there surely is not a better site for a public building. Architecturally, it is an extremely challenging site, too. Jutting out into the shipping channels of the Harbour, with Sydney Cove to the west and Farm Cove to the east, it is surrounded on three sides by water. On the fourth side is the city and the Botanical Gardens. To the west, and above it is the roadway of the Sydney Harbour Bridge. What this meant to an architect designing a building for the site was that whatever was built there had to look good not from just one side, as would a building going into a street of other buildings, but it had to be visually appealing from five sides. People would watch it from the harbour and suburbs opposite on three sides, from the foot of Bennelong Point (the fourth side) and from the Harbour Bridge and some of the city's taller buildings, looking down (the fifth side).

Finishing touches to a bar with a view.

What the judges saw when they examined Utzon's drawings during those days in 1957 was a building which fulfilled this need perfectly. The great arching sails would, indeed, be visually appealing as well as imposing from five different aspects.

And the design married with the setting, too. Some people saw Utzon's roof vaults as sails, others as shells and others as waves. Whichever way they saw it, for most people, the atmosphere created by Utzon's design was a maritime atmosphere.

Design to Fit the Site

Two of the design imprints of Utzon's generation of architects are a strong feeling for landscape and the architectural environment and a fascination with horizontal planes, or platforms, as a major design element. What the young Dane proposed for Bennelong Point was to transform the point into a massive concrete platform or podium and on this to erect a series of soaring roof vaults, white in colour and gracefully curved so that in no way would they be at odds with their environment. And, with further sympathy for the Bennelong Point environment, he planned to enclose the vaults with glass which would virtually allow the environment to enter the building and eliminate any vertical-plane mass to clash with the graceful form of the whole. One distinguished commentator said of the design that he had correlated a high rise building with a cosmic expanse of sea and sky.

At the same time Utzon had solved a number of the major problems set by the site. On his concrete platform covering four and a half acres of a fairly narrow promontory Utzon planned to build, side by side, two separate theatres, each enclosed by its own series of shells. Slightly forward of these he planned another separate set of shells to enclose a main restaurant. Each of the theatres was to be a single-storeyed structure with the seating placed on top of the podium and most of the ancillary functions deep inside this concrete base. The roof vaults would enclose, dome-like, all the functional elements, including the stage towers.

One of the major problems confronting most of the entrants in the design competition was to actually fit the two main auditoria on to the narrow site. For most, the solution was to place their theatres back to back, along the site. This left plenty of room for movement of people around the perimeter of the building and it also offered a design solution for the problem of disguising the stage towers, which could be then contained in a single aesthetic structure. But it posed the problem of acoustically isolating the two theatres. When performances were going on in both theatres at the same time it was possible that the sound from one performance would interrupt the other. By placing his theatres side by side in separate but integrated structures Utzon had eliminated this acoustical interference.

Another drawback to the back-to-back concept was that people entering the landward theatres would not have the same opportunity to enjoy the vista of the harbour that was so much a vital element of the site's environment as would those who were entering the theatre at the harbour end of the site. The flow of people entering what was intended to be a total cultural complex would be interrupted as soon as it reached the site. There would be two major flows of people on to the site, heading for two theatres whose entrances were a considerable distance from each other. By placing the theatres side by side with one major integrated entry point — the vast staircase leading up the outside of the podium to the theatre shells and its interior twin, the vehicle concourse and stairway — Utzon provided for a unified flow of people.

Once inside the complex — because Utzon had placed both stages at the landward end of the point — audiences would move around the outside of the auditoria, past the stages, to the entry foyers at the harbour end, where every theatregoer would have the opportunity to enjoy the building's marriage with sky and water.

In addition, because of this smooth flow of people along the wide corridors and because the single-storey design had eliminated the need for many separate staircases, there would be no people-jam in the case of an emergency. The theatres could be emptied quickly and smoothly as people left by a number of doors into corridors or foyers that would lead them directly outside.

Stage towers are always an aesthetic problem for theatre designers. Every theatre must have a tall tower to enclose the complex network of scenery and backdrops, known as the flies, and this is usually fairly easily designed in a theatre which fits into a streetscape — the tower is at the back of the theatre, abutting its rear neighbour and therefore out of sight from the street. But because of the five-way view of the Opera House the stage tower presented special visual problems. Utzon had overcome this with the soaring sculpture of his roof vaults.

Thus he had effectively eliminated noise interference between the neighbouring theatres, provided a most efficient and safe flow of people and vehicles to the narrow site, afforded every theatre-goer the opportunity to take in the most spectacular view from any theatre in the world, and effectively concealed the stage towers. All of this in a most imposing and imaginative piece of architectural sculpture. The judges had been impressed almost to the point of awe by their selection. For they had based their choice on the simplest of drawings; on a concept rather than on a design. And in so doing they had overlooked or minimised some of the problems presented by the concept — for example, the lack of wing space caused by placing the two stages side by side on the podium (a problem which has become one of the major criticisms of performers in the opera theatre).

Deep inside the podium: the access tunnel and storage area between the Opera Theatre and the Concert Hall.

Utzon explained something of his concept later, when he wrote: 'The Sydney Opera House is one of those buildings where the roof is of major importance. It is a house which is completely exposed. The Sydney Opera House is a house which one will see from above, will sail around, because it sits on a point sticking out into a harbour, a very beautiful harbour, a fjord with a lot of inlets. This point is in the middle of the city and the city rises on both sides of the fjord so the Opera House is a focal point. This means that one could not design a building for such an exposed position without paying attention to the roof. One could not have a flat roof filled with ventilation pipes — in fact one must have a fifth facade which is just as important as the other facades. Furthermore, people will sail around it, there are ferries sailing past and large ships coming in — the big harbour is just outside and the large bridge nearby, so people will see it as a round thing. They will not see it as a house in a street, either along the street or across.

'Therefore, instead of making a square form, I have made a sculpture — a sculpture covering the necessary functions, in other words the rooms express themselves, the size of the rooms is expressed in these roofs. If you think of a Gothic church, you are closer to what I have been aiming at. Looking at a Gothic church you never get tired, you will never be finished with it — when you pass around it or see it against the sky. It is as if something new goes on all the time and it is so important — this interplay is so important that together with the sun, the light and clouds, it makes a living thing.'

In a brief note, Utzon explained his entry to the judging panel in much the same terms as they had used in giving their reasons for choosing it.

'The architecture emphasises the character of Bennelong Point and takes the greatest advantage of the view. The approach of the audience is easy and as distinctly pronounced as in Grecian theatres by uncomplicated staircase construction. There is a clear distinction between the different functions in regard to sound, fire regulations and theatrical technique as well as between audience, actors and stage technicians. The solution of one-storeyed depressed side-stages solves the difficult acoustics of the stage technicians during performance.'

Fire regulations had been met by direct access on to terraces from any room in any storey on the Opera House. Dead space for fire escapes had thus been eliminated.

'Covered connections between all parts of the building have been provided for. Light, suspended concrete shells accentuate the plateau effect and the character of the staircase constructions,' Utzon said.

'The remainder of the site would retain a stone character similar to that which already existed,' he added.

But it was the sculptural aspect of Utzon's concept that first caught the eye of the judges — for, in fact, there was little else to capture their attention.

A sketch by Utzon which shows one of his earliest concepts of the Opera House as a curved, cloud-like structure floating above a platform.

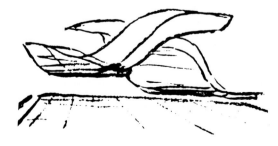

In their report on the winning design the judges said this: 'The drawings submitted are simple to the point of being diagrammatic. Nevertheless, as we have returned again and again to the study of these drawings we are convinced that they present a concept of an Opera House which is capable of being one of the great buildings of the world. Because of its very originality, it is clearly a controversial design. We are, however, absolutely convinced about its merits. A massive base emphasises the character of Bennelong Point. The auditoria are arranged like Greek theatres in this rising base and are approached either underground from cars or externally along a magnificent ceremonial approach. This approach and the auditoria steps form a rising plateau in which the highest point of seating is about 40 feet above the ground. This conception solves by elimination all the complex needs of (emergency) escape which form so much dead space in a multi-storey building.

'While this scheme substantially conforms to the conditions laid down, we are aware that it is open to many points of detailed criticism and a number of corrections would have to be made (a rearrangement of dressing rooms and rehearsal areas was envisaged), but we feel that at this stage the general breadth of the imaginative concept is an over-riding consideration.'

Earlier, in a circumspect interview about their still secret choice, the judges made these comments: 'Predominantly, most of the competitors tried to solve the problem in today's techniques. We looked for a monumental work. After all, you don't go to the opera very often. It is a bit of an occasion and it's nice to go to a magnificent building. That's why we kept in mind that the Opera House design had to be an imaginative thing.'

They had been impressed, then, not only with the visual imagination, but also with the structural imagination Utzon had displayed.

Later, Professor Ashworth, who had been a member of the judging panel, added: 'While it is the assessors' duty to ensure that all things considered, the winning scheme is the best solution to the problem, they in their turn hope that among the schemes submitted will be one which in the widest sense will help to forward the development of the architecture of our time. I think that Sydney has proved fortunate in that just such a scheme was in fact among the entries submitted.

'Obviously an opera house is a very special kind of building — one that may be erected but once in a century or two and which thus becomes a landmark as it were, expressive of the architecture of its day and age. While we can appreciate the famous Paris Opera, La Scala in Milan and, of more recent date, the well-known theatres in Utrecht and Malmo, the Festival Hall in London and the University Theatre in Massachusetts, what a great disaster and disappointment it would have been if this challenge to Australia generally and architecture in particular, had resulted in another revival of a bygone age or,

even worse, in a pedestrian building, guaranteed not even to evoke criticism.

'We have then a fine site and the opportunity to place upon it a great significant building worthy of the best possible effort any architect could make. All the assessors were of the opinion that it was particularly important to realise that any building placed upon the site would be seen from all around the harbour and in many cases from a high level — thus the building must look well from almost any point of view. Professor Denis Winston has already said that the 'winning design gives the impression of a wonderful piece of sculpture deliberately placed to be seen from all points of view,' and this opinion expresses exactly the assessors' initial consideration.

'For this reason the assessors considered that the placing of large, massive, box-like buildings, however practical, upon this particular site would be wrong. It was felt that the building must have unity, a sense of movement and should preferably build up towards the point thrusting out with the harbour. Thus the assessors considered that the first essential requirement should be a magnificent general concept — the fact that any building must function was of course accepted as a sine qua non. Einstein once said 'perfection of means and confusion of aims seems to be characteristic of our age.' Our aim in this instance, I submit, was to find a fine piece of imaginative architecture — the means comprise a secondary issue.'

Ironically, the assessors had also been impressed with the price of Utzon's building. Soon after Utzon's win had been announced Professor Ashworth said that quantitative surveyors had examined the 10 leading entries in the design competition and had reported that the winner was by far the cheapest to build.

An estimate of about $7 million was given that January 29.

It did not — largely because of the conceptual view of the assessors, explained above, and also because the judges had not been given a cost ceiling within which to work — foresee the difficulties that were to come.

But Premier Cahill, that day, seemed to have some premonition of the troubles that were to face him and his successors.

'The assessors have already stated that they expect some criticism of the design they have chosen,' he said.

'It is not my intention to enter the lists on that score at any time. I shall leave controversy of that nature to those better qualified than myself. On the other hand there has been, and doubtless will be, some criticism of the project itself, of the site which the government has chosen, of the wisdom of building an opera house at all, and of the community's ability to shoulder the expense of maintaining a National Opera House. Those are the things which crop up from day to day and are something that the government and I will have to face.

'I would do no more than refer critics of the chosen site to the opinion of the assessors. The problem of whether or not such a project should be attempted at this time is one that concerns the government more immediately. That there is a real need for a building of this type can be deduced from the rapidly growing interest, not only in every aspect of the theatre itself, but in the performance of serious music and ballet.

'It is equally certain that there is not one theatre or hall in Sydney which can even remotely approach modern requirements for the large-scale presentation of music, choral works, opera or ballet. That this state of affairs should exist in a city of nearly two million is regrettable.

'To those who say that this is not the time to commence such a project I would say that to postpone a decision would turn an immediately desirable work into an urgent necessity in the not too distant future. In the meantime, music and theatre in this country would be in danger of languishing through lack of official encouragement, and suitable sites would become a fast diminishing commodity. I am sure that most will agree that the government's decision was not rash or ill-considered.'

His speech gave not only an indication of the wily Cahill's perception that there was political trouble to come over the design and construction of the Opera House, but also of his desire to push the project ahead with all possible speed — a desire that was to be the root cause of many of the difficulties he had foreshadowed.

Utzon Goes to Work

Newspapers in those days still found it necessary to boast a little when they made an overseas telephone call. So the fact that they had actually interviewed Utzon by a radio-telephone call to Hellebaek, Denmark, was almost as big a piece of news as the interview itself. Few people knew who Utzon was, let alone anything about him, so the interviews largely rested on 'colourful' stuff about his height and the size of his family and how he imagined the sunshine in Sydney. Reporters who telephoned Utzon said they could hear champagne glasses clinking in the background.

Indeed, on that January 29, 1957, Utzon was celebrating his win in the design competition, with champagne. He had never expected to win. He told reporters he was inspired to his design by many beautiful pictures of Bennelong Point and the harbour ('It must be one of the most beautiful spots in the world. I have dreamt of it so much. Then came the idea with that roof. Do they like it in Sydney?')

He said he would use the prize-money to bring his whole family to Australia, depending on how long he would have to stay ('An opera house is not built in a day you know — not even in Sydney.')

He was very, very happy with the win and his wife was just as thrilled with the win as he was ('We have three children. A boy aged 12, a girl aged 10 and our baby son who was born on New Year's Day this year. This news from Australia is almost as good as the news of his arrival.')

Utzon said he had won 20 architectural prizes before but this one was the most important. He had spent about six months from May to December 1956 working on the design 'whenever I could get time off from my other work.'

Utzon, apparently, laughed a booming laugh quite often during the interview.

But the laughter and celebration was soon over because Utzon, while a visionary and a man who believes in pushing concepts to the limits of the possible, is also a practical man. He had won the contest and that, according to the terms set down in Sydney, meant he was already the design architect, responsible for bringing to reality the vision he had so sketchily proposed in his entry. (There were a few elevations of the building and plans of a couple of levels of the podium, some details such as what the seats should look like and how the podium should be faced with stone and some overall views. There was little else.)

Translating the concept of the sweeping shell roofs into a structural reality would, in the truest sense, be pushing a concept to the limits of the possible.

Under the terms of the competition Utzon had won $10,000 and he would be paid a further $60,000 if work on the Opera House did not begin within two years. He had won previous competitions and with this money and the guaranteed fee, whether work proceeded or not, he was able to finance an immediate start on developing his concept.

He shunned all other work to concentrate on producing more detailed drawings of the Opera House. In this he worked in concert with an associate, Erik Andersson, a Swede whose office was in the town of Halsingborg, a few miles from Hellebaek, across the narrow strip of water that separates Denmark from Sweden. Andersson and Utzon had worked together before in a number of design competitions and, in fact, Andersson had collaborated to a degree on the first drawings of the Opera House. But in the Opera House project, Utzon had taken over most of the design and the entry was submitted in his name. This was in agreement with their arrangement that the partner who did most work on a design should attach his name to it.

Utzon settled down immediately to developing his original drawings and building a model (he was a great believer in using models to explain his ideas).

In Sydney there was agitation for Utzon to come and accept his prize and give a detailed explanation of the prize-winning design. But the architect chose to remain in Denmark, working. He would not come to Sydney, he said, until the government had officially told him that work on the Opera House would go ahead.

He had developed a concept and one which was admired by the international judges, that was clear. Now he had to make it work. There would be much thinking, much discussion and much drawing ahead.

Finance and Utzon's First Visit

Up to the announcement of Utzon as the prizewinner, the Opera House project had been virtually a one-man show, that of the Premier J. J. Cahill. He had been able to push through the idea of building the Opera House with only a little trouble. But now Sydney had a site for an opera house and it had a design for one. Now it needed the finance — and that needed popular support.

From the moment Cahill announced the winner of the design competition, three arguments of almost equal intensity broke out in Sydney and continued to rage unabated. They were over the design itself; over what the building should be called (the Sydney Morning Herald suggested a consensus of its readers would like it to be the Bennelong Pavilion, housing Queen's Hall and Prince's Theatre); and over finance.

Cahill, up to now, had never mentioned the cost of building the Opera House in anything but the vaguest and most general terms. He had said quantity surveyors thought the Utzon design would cost the equivalent of about $7 million. But he made no firm commitment to cost. He had, however, made a very firm commitment — especially to himself — to build the Opera House. To back down on this commitment would show him up in a weak light and Cahill did not want this, quite naturally. In fact, what Cahill wanted was a start made on the Opera House construction well before the election, two years away. The conditions of the design competition said that construction had to begin within two years of the winner being announced. It could be easily inferred from this that Cahill intended that the start of work on the building would be the crown piece of his election platform.

Now his political guile was to be put to the test in devising a method of financing this Opera House — a cultural indulgence, as so many New South Wales voters regarded it. In the late 1950s there was a decided housing shortage in New South Wales, property values were climbing and the people, like all Australians chasing that increasingly elusive dream of a cottage on their own quarter-acre, might be angered if money which could have been spent on housing was diverted to an opera house which many saw as the preserve of an elite few. Cahill had allowed the misnomer Opera House to stick with the project and this always conjured up elitist visions in the minds of many egalitarian Australians.

Had Cahill firmly announced, very early in the piece, that the building would be called the Sydney Entertainment Centre (cultural might have brought on an elitist picture, too) or some other such general name which more suited the aims of the project, his task of financing it might have been less difficult politically.

As it was he and some others had suggested at one stage that it be called the National Opera House, thus implying it was a national cultural centre and that as such the Federal Government in Canberra should play a part in financing it. But this was probably a little optimistic — particularly in view of the continuing rivalry between Sydney and Melbourne who had always vied for the title of Australia's premier city. It would also have been somewhat hypocritical. Cahill had seen his project among other things, as a poke in Melbourne's proud cultural eye.

The letters pages of the newspapers were filled with suggestions for financing the building, from advance sales of seats to a tax on those who liked opera and the Opera House.

Two things became clear to Cahill — there was little hope of the Commonwealth Government helping him out with the cost and, while there was great support for the project, there was widespread opposition to it as a piece of extravagance when State finance was badly needed in many other areas. To build it from State revenue would be political suicide, especially for a Labor Government which had a power base of trade unions whose members would, largely, see an opera house as a rich man's playground.

Cahill had to devise some method of financing that was as imaginative as the design of the building. He did.

Ten days after the announcement of Utzon's win Cahill mentioned the idea of running a special State lottery to raise the funds for construction. There was little reaction to the idea at the time. It went almost unnoticed and, since it was an unsourced leak when it appeared as a news story, it was probably largely regarded as a piece of press speculation. However, it was one method of financing the project which was considered along with many others by the Opera House Committee that February. But most attention was being directed towards some form of public appeal for funds to start the project at least while the Premier worked out some system of financing.

In the meantime Cahill worked at building public acceptance of the project itself, and publicly at least, did not raise the idea of a lottery again for some time. He dealt with people who opposed the concept of an opera house, those who thought it an unnecessary luxury. And he played his politics hard. At one stage he lamented that the Opera House probably never would be built and this seemed to have the desired effect. The press leapt in and criticised him. Sydney DID want an opera house he was told. Well, he replied, the Government was still hopeful.

But there was still much opposition to the project, even among Cahill's backbench Labor Party members in the State Parliament. Cahill assessed the opposition as being strong enough to kill the project because he deferred putting the question to his party (whose approval was necessary before the project could be given the force of law). About the same time Cahill said he doubted that Sydney would ever have its Opera House, Professor Ashworth joined in the argument and urged the urgent launching of an appeal for funds from the public. This, he said, would test public opinion about the Opera House. He added that he thought Cahill was still intent on pushing ahead with the plan.

John Coburn's magnificent Curtain of the Sun in the Opera Theatre.

John Coburn's magnificent Curtain of the Sun in the Opera Theatre.

Coburn's colourful Curtain of the Moon in the Drama Theatre.

Indeed, he was. On May 1, 1957 Cahill again raised his idea of a special State lottery. He put it in specific terms: four lotteries a year, each ticket to cost $3 and first prize to be $100,000. This would raise about $900,000 towards the cost of the Opera House in the two years before construction began and a little after. He also told his parliamentary colleagues that a public appeal would be launched, the State Government would make a contribution from general revenue of $200,000 and there would be contributions from the City Council and the Commonwealth Government through the Australian Broadcasting Commission (which would be the biggest user of the Opera House through its sponsorship of the Sydney Symphony Orchestra and visiting performers). The lotteries, Cahill proposed, would continue until the Opera House was paid for.

The reaction was pretty much as Cahill expected. Of course, there was opposition to the idea of using gambling to pay for the Opera House. But generally the scheme was received with approval. Australians, especially those in New South Wales where poker machines claim millions of dollars annually, are avid gamblers. Another form of State approved gambling, an extension of the existing State lottery, would not hurt. Newspapers pointed out the objections to such a scheme but approved it as the most practical means of raising the finance. And they praised Cahill for his vigor and tenacity in advancing the scheme.

The fact that it would put almost no strain on the State's resources made it pretty hard for critics to advance a sound practical argument. Even the moral argument was weak. The government's answer to this was that gamblers would be at least doing something constructive with their money.

A week later the Parliamentary Labor Party approved an early start to building and the launching of a public appeal for funds. It gave tacit approval to the lottery scheme. But in order to make sure his position was totally secure — especially from attack within his own party — Cahill decided to defer a decision until the project had been approved by the State Labor Party's highest policy-making body, the State Conference. A month later, on June 16, the conference endorsed the project. Then, on July 3, the parliamentary Labor members reiterated their approval.

Pushing the scheme through Parliament became merely a formality. The conference endorsement made the project an official policy which all members of the State party were bound to support. Cahill announced that day that a public appeal for funds would be launched and that a final decision on the lottery would be made soon.

He also announced that Utzon would be invited to come to Sydney as soon as possible. The government would proceed immediately with plans to build the Opera House.

Utzon arrived at Sydney Airport on the night of July 29, 1957, with his partner Erik Andersson. Utzon was pressed for some enlightenment on his design and its inspiration. He told the crowd of

Coburn's colourful Curtain of the Moon in the Drama Theatre.

reporters: 'We had no trouble visualising Bennelong Point because we have the castle of Elsinore (the same as in Macbeth) on the point just like your tram depot at Fort Macquarie. We could look at the castle and just visualise the Opera House.'

Early the next day Utzon toured the site on Bennelong Point for the first time. He said: 'It's absolutely breathtaking. There's no opera house site in the world to compare with it.' His first impression had not been affected by the bleak and windy weather that whipped up the harbour around the point.

Discussions with the Premier and other officials followed the site inspection and Utzon agreed to some changes in the original design: the seating in the main hall was to be reduced from 3500 to 3000 to avoid the use of balconies; Utzon was to suggest how best to provide for an opera audience of not less than 1700 or more than 2000; seating in the small hall was to be limited to 1200 for dramatic performances.

The Sydney Daily Telegraph reported: "The Under-Secretary for Local Government (Mr Haviland), who is chairman of the Opera House Executive Committee, said last night the Committee had asked Mr Utzon to make these changes.'

This means that as early as 1957, on Utzon's first visit to Australia, those most closely associated with directing the project were having second thoughts about what precisely was wanted in the building. They seemed small enough and reasonable enough changes in those heady days of the launching. Let's be sure and let's get it right, seemed to be the attitude. But in hindsight these small changes were merely a foretaste of much bigger things to come — and things for which many people have blamed Utzon and accused him of a lack of planning.

As a result of his discussions with Utzon, Cahill made the announcement he had been most anxious to make — the basis for his desire to get Utzon to Australia: the foundation stone of the Sydney Opera House would be laid, he said, before the State elections due in 1959.

Demolition of the tram sheds on Bennelong Point would begin and the site would be ready for construction within 18 months, he announced on July 30. Cahill said he had put this timetable to Utzon and Andersson and Utzon had said: 'Alright. We will do it.'

At the same time Cahill announced that the Government had approved the appointment of Ove Arup and Partners as structural engineers for the project. Utzon, in fact, had already had some preliminary discussions with Arup, the distinguished Danish-English engineer who is now Sir Ove, and had asked the State Government to appoint his firm.

When they flew out of Sydney on August 21, 1957 for Denmark via Japan and the United States, Utzon and Andersson seemed perfectly happy with their visit. They planned to be back in March the following year with more plans and ready for detailed discussions with the technical committee of the

Fort Macquarie tramsheds.

Utzon, Andersson and Professor Ashworth inspect the site on the Dane's first visit to Australia.

Opera House executive. There was no problem with the changes in seating arrangements they had been asked to make. There was no reason, they said, why construction of the Opera House could not begin as announced by the Premier, within 18 months.

More Money, More Details

The next few months for Utzon and his team in Hellebaek were feverish. And they were pretty hectic in Sydney too — a city flushed with the anticipation of work beginning on its great cultural pleasure-dome. The public appeal for funds had been launched at the Town Hall on August 7, when Utzon was still in Australia. At this meeting of top citizens Cahill handed over a cheque for $200,000 to the Opera House Committee — the State Government's promised contribution. Then followed what must have seemed like something of an orgy in the overtly prim days of Sydney in the late 1950s. Some of the city's distinguished women began to sell kisses.

Utzon's partner, Andersson, offered $100 for the right to kiss the Australian operatic darling Joan Hammond and then, not to be outdone, Utzon paid a similar sum to kiss Elaine Shaffer, the flautist. And Elaine Shaffer paid $20 to kiss Charles Moses, chief of the Australian Broadcasting Commission who was so flattered by Miss Shaffer's desire that he gave $100 to the fund anyway.

In this sense of gaiety several of the city's citizens pledged large sums to the appeal and Cahill's own imaginative scheme for financing the building was under way. Three days later the appeal had raised almost $500,000.

On September 26, he announced his scheme to run a special State lottery. The government had considered the scheme (it had also considered that the cost of the Opera House was going to be considerably more than the $7 million originally mentioned) and decided to boost the major prize to the equivalent of $200,000 and the price of a ticket to $10.

'The whole thing is deplorable,' said the Coadjutor Bishop of Sydney, the Right Reverend W. G. Hilliard. 'It is regrettable that a government should be financing a cultural movement by the encouragement of a social vice.'

But the arguments in favour were too strong. There was no pressure on the public purse and Australian gamblers would, while enjoying their flutter, produce quite happily some $1 million a year for the building of the Opera House.

In the months that followed, the public responded fairly generously to the Opera House fund — though not as generously as had been hoped.

Utzon, in the meantime, working long hours with added staff in Denmark was producing a lavish document which he would bring to Sydney in March 1958 to explain his design in much greater detail. On his way back from his first visit to Sydney he had talked with Ove Arup and preliminary investigations

Andersson, Utzon, Ashworth and Sir Charles Moses. Behind them is Unilever House, one of Sydney's first curtain walled buildings.

of the roof design were under way. Utzon was busy not only developing his plans but also engaging specialist consultants.

He planned to do most of his preliminary design work in Denmark so he hired Danish consultants who were, it just turned out, also among the top men in their fields, if not the top. Apart from Arup he engaged Dr Vilhelm Jordan as an acoustics consultant, J. Varming as consultant on mechanical services, M. Balslev as consultant on electrical installations and Sandro Malmquist as consultant on theatre techniques. With the help of these people the original spare sketches of the Utzon concept were being fleshed out.

Utzon, for example, was taking a special interest in how the tiles to glaze the shells would be made to suit his needs and how they would be eventually fixed to the shells so that there was absolute uniformity. It was at this stage that he devised the system eventually used of prefabricating giant lids of tiles on the ground and hoisting them to the roof shells where they were fixed on with a complex bracket system.

Ove Arup and Partners were looking at ways in which the roof system could be made to stand up. In conferences in London, Utzon had indicated that he would be prepared to change the shape of the shells in order to make them work. Such was the enormity of the engineering problems detected in the design so early in the piece. Dr Jordan was advising Utzon and his staff on acoustical problems raised by the design. After all, if the building had poor acoustics and it admitted extraneous sounds from the harbour during performances it would not be worth going on with.

Malmquist was working on one of the toughest problems apart from making the roofs stand up. The Utzon design, by placing the two theatres side by side on Bennelong Point, left very little wing space for the operation of scenery that in most theatres can be wheeled on and off the stage in minutes. He began to think of ignoring conventional methods of stage operation. It was decided that the best way around the problem was to make the stage in the main hall work vertically. Stage scenery could be operated on a system of strip elevators which would raise scenery from below the stage level.

This was the flesh of the earliest design and was the chief work which was to be published in the elaborate and elegant Red Book, Utzon's first detailed explanation of how his concept would work. Back in Sydney, plans went ahead on the finance. The first of the Opera House Lotteries was launched on November 25.

But after the strong starting burst in which almost $500,000 was raised, the appeal was beginning to flag.

The first lottery was drawn on January 10, 1958. Tickets were held by people in Britain, the United States, Canada, South Africa, New Zealand, Fiji and New Guinea. But the winner was a wealthy Sydney businessman, Mr Oswald Sellers, the owner of an advertising agency and a director of another advertising agency, a chocolate company, a grocery firm and a sheep station. He lived at sumptuous Point Piper in a mansion with a gardener, chauffeur and housekeeper.

The lottery had raised $320,000 for the Opera House fund. Lottery number two was launched almost immediately but, because it was holiday time it was explained, sales did not go as well as expected. Then in late March, when the third lottery was being sold, Cahill announced that no more would be held until the end of the year. Subscriptions were slow and the big ones had affected sales of other State lotteries.

About the same time Utzon returned to Sydney, his gloriously produced Red Book (24 in by 15 in) tucked under his arm. He was in Sydney to tell the city how he would build his Opera House. And although the Red Book was more a piece of masterful public relations publishing than a document of working drawings it did help to fill in many gaps.

Utzon brought Ove Arup with him to explain some of the structural problems and solutions in the long series of meetings that had been scheduled, especially with the Technical Committee. In addition to the Red Book they brought a series of other plans and models.

'I have been doing nothing but eat, sleep and work on the house with a lot of people at the office,' Utzon told an interviewer. 'And now we know how it will be built.'

He was thumbing through a copy of the Red Book as he lounged one morning in his Bondi motel room. 'When you enter you get a feeling you don't get in any other house,' he said.

'The roof and the walls are one thing; you can't say where the one starts and the other ends. When I was in London, Mr Jenkins, who is Mr Arup's partner, took me to a blackboard in his office. It was covered with mathematical formulas describing the shells of the house. Can't you see the beauty of it!'

In the Red Book, Arup and Partners had recommended extensive model testing of the roofs. Some minor alterations had been necessary to the shape of the roofs but they remained, the report said, generally unchanged from Utzon's original concept. The surfaces of the shells had been defined geometrically (each would rise in quite a sharp curve and flatten out as it neared its peak). Nothing was solved but Arup and Partners knew, or thought they knew, where they were heading.

'By thus defining the surfaces,' Arup wrote, 'a basis has been created for the calculation of the forces acting on the shells and the stresses created in the shells.'

He pointed out that these would be considerable and that it had been decided to strengthen each roof shell with a series of ribs fanning out from the two supporting points at the base and meeting in a ridge at the top. Also it had been decided to make the glass infills in each shell load-bearing membranes. (This would have had the effect of joining up the shells. The plan was later abandoned because engineers later saw the possibility of a sort of domino effect if the shells were interconnected, so that if one shell fell the rest would follow it.)

Arup concluded: 'Extensive model tests will be required to arrive at a true distribution of stresses under varying loads.'

In his notes, Dr Jordan, the acoustics consultant, recommended an early start to acoustic model tests. He pointed out that the main hall would have a volume of 390 cubic feet per seat with an audience of 2800 and a volume of 360 cubic feet per seat with an audience of 1800. This compared with what Dr Jordan said was generally regarded as an ideal acoustic volume of 360 cubic feet per seat.

These are important figures in Opera House history. In his Red Book notes Dr Jordan pointed out that corresponding figures for other major performing auditoria around the world were: London's Royal Festival Hall (often said to have the finest concert acoustics in the world) 228; Amsterdam's Concertgebouw 322, Copenhagen's Tivoli Concert Hall 253, Edinburgh's Usher Hall 200. What Utzon had been working towards with these volumes was a successful dual purpose concert hall and opera theatre under the main shell with a reverberation time of 1.7 seconds, which he and Jordan believed would be capable of electronic variation so that it would favour whichever was being performed, concert or opera.

Nobody seems to have objected in 1958 to these aims — the production of a dual purpose hall with a universally satisfactory reverberation time. At those 1958 meetings were senior representatives of the Australian Broadcasting Commission, the Australian Elizabethan Theatre Trust (parent of the Australian Opera Company), and Hoyt's Theatres (the cinema group). The ABC was to become the major user of the Opera House for symphony concerts and the Australian Opera Company for opera performances.

In 1966 the ABC's new general manager Talbot Duckmanton said it was impossible to build an acoustically satisfactory dual purpose hall — a statement from which stemmed the most traumatic change of plans in the whole of the Opera House's history. Back in 1958, however, at those early meetings the original idea of a major hall to be used for both symphony concerts and opera was being pursued and happily by both the Opera House Committee and Utzon and his acoustical adviser.

The one acoustical concern expressed came when Utzon proposed his solution to the problems he had been asked to solve back in late 1957 — restricting the size of the major hall to 3000 for concerts, providing a means of accommodating an opera audience of between 1700 and 2000 in either hall and finding a way of limiting the seating in the minor hall to 1200 for dramatic performances.

Utzon proposed to provide 2702 seats in the main hall without a balcony and 3000 with a balcony. This would be for concerts. For opera performances he planned seating of 1826. He and Sandro Malmquist, the consultant on theatre techniques, had devised a way of extending the stage area for opera and of reducing it to provide the extra seating for concerts. Acoustics were raised when Sir Charles Moses (then Mr) of the ABC said he preferred to have the larger audience provided by a balcony but for acoustical reasons he was prepared to forego the extra revenue it would reap. Eventually, it was agreed there would be a maximum of 2800 seats for concerts and 1700 for opera in a main hall without balconies. There would be 1200 seats in the small hall and balconies would be used to keep the audience as close to the stage as possible. The committee also asked Utzon to provide a 400-seat experimental theatre down inside the podium and he agreed to do this.

Another detail touched on in the Red Book by Malmquist was the extraordinarily tricky one of the lack of side stage space caused by Utzon's placement of the two halls side by side on the point. Malmquist (who was replaced by Dr Walter Unruh, the distinguished stage designer who had worked on, for example, the Lincoln Centre in New York, almost immediately after the presentation of the Red Book) wrote: 'Until the last few decades the stage had in principle not been subject to any change for 200 years or more — apart from development of the technical auxiliary equipment. Now it is no longer so. We have broken out of the snailshell of the baroque theatre and have discovered so many more ways to play theatre. That is why it seems the only right and natural thing to the theatre's artistic leaders, to stage managers and producers, that a theatre that is built nowadays must be so constructed that it is not tied down firmly to one playhouse form, but that it is a theatre house that lives and that can change from an architectonic atmosphere according to the changing theatrical forms whose development it makes possible. The play stages housed within the Sydney Opera and Theatre House should fill most of the demands that can be made for this purpose.'

He went on to describe the function of the unique vertically operated stage machinery system he had designed to overcome the lack of side space. The point that the Red Book made most strongly was that the spirit of innovation set by Utzon's original concept had not been compromised in its development, either by Utzon or by his consultants.

What had been compromised to a certain extent was the seating capacity. Originally, the design competition had called for a dual purpose theatre seating between 3000 and 3500 and a drama theatre seating at least 1200. Now this was being held down to 2800 for the big hall and restricted to a maximum of 1200 for the small hall. The people responsible for the project in Sydney would have liked more time to rethink their original requirements and firm up, once and for all, what was to be built on Bennelong Point.

But Joe Cahill was not a man for compromise. While new arguments over the compromise seating capacities raged Cahill pressed ahead with characteristic single-mindedness. After discussions with Utzon that March in 1958 he announced that

Above the broadwalk there is another walk, where the shells meet the podium, with spectacular views.
The world's biggest pillarless vehicle concourse.

work would begin on his Opera House a year later. Nothing would stop him, was the implicit message in his announcement. Cahill knew he had an election soon after March 1959, he knew that the beginning of work would be the centrepiece of his platform and he knew that if the pace of the project was allowed to slow down now or lapse, it could be lost forever — certainly for his election campaign.

Utzon returned to Denmark to his increasingly intricate problems, notably working with Arup and Partners to make the roofs stand up and then stay there in high winds. The Opera House Committee set about the task of finding the people to carry out Cahill's wishes. They decided to split the project into stages and call tenders for the first, stage, the construction of the podium. This would mean that Cahill's demands for an early start would be satisfied and time would be bought. But at what price?

Engineers began sinking test bores on Bennelong Point on May 11, 1958. They were in search of bedrock for the foundations. At the same time acoustics tests began on the site to obtain information about wind velocities and traffic noises.

By now the public appeal for funds was well and truly flagging. There was some talk of engaging professional fund raisers to see if they could reverse the position that had arisen — that the fund was costing more to administer than it was raising. The great lottery, which had been postponed earlier in the year because of its effect on other State lotteries was to be revived. (It was revived, for only three more draws before being dropped again.) But this was no time for such mundane matters as finance. Utzon was on his way to call tenders for the first work and Cahill was preparing to lay the foundation stone in only a few months. The wreckers moved on to Bennelong Point on August 18 and the old tram sheds began to tumble.

Utzon arrived in Australia on November 3, 1958. He brought with him Mr J. Varming, the air conditioning and mechanical specialist, and Mr Balslev, the electrical installations consultant. They were followed a few days later by Jenkins, the senior partner in Arup's London office. Utzon also brought with him detailed plans of the podium section and a number of models, including one the size of a living room which had been used for acoustical tests and another which showed the auditoria as he wanted them built. The plans he brought with him were to be the basis on which tenders would be called for the first real work on construction.

Utzon said on his arrival: 'We are now confident that the new Opera House building will be a great success.'

At the same time Haviland, chairman of the Opera House committee, announced the first in the long series of cost escalations. The building would now cost $9.6 million, not $7.4 million as originally estimated. Elevators, the experimental theatre and other modifications had caused the increase, he said. In the enthusiasm, his statement hardly caused a ripple.

Foyer-passages like this one provide access to the auditoria through several doors and lead to the harbourside foyers.

Six companies were invited to submit tenders and Jenkins arrived to study their qualifications. Utzon returned to his work in Denmark and London.

In the meantime Actors' Equity and the National Pensioners' Society had looked at the initial cost estimate and the first of the increases and decided that the Opera House was not worth the money. The pensioners sought legal action to prevent its construction and the actors suggested a greater spread of the money to benefit the arts more generally. On opening day in 1973 Equity was still opposed to the Opera House.

Tenders closed on January 19. The six firms seeking to build the podium had quoted between $2.7 million and $4.4 million and the Opera House Committee decided to accept the lowest — that of Civil and Civic, run by a Dutch engineer named Gerardus Dusseldorp, who has since become one of Australia's wealthiest men and one of the biggest property developers through his Lend Lease organisation. The project for which he was to build the foundations on Bennelong Point defies superlatives as a property development.

Construction Begins

Drizzling rain fell from a low bank of dark clouds as 400 people gathered on Bennelong Point on the afternoon of March 2, 1959, to watch Premier Cahill lay a plaque to mark the start of construction. Utzon had designed the bronze plaque and brought it with him to Sydney a few days earlier.

It was to be placed on a sandstone plinth which represented the first step in the great stairway leading to the entrance of the building and would mark the spot from which all measurements on the site would be taken.

The timing of the ceremony was politically perfect for Cahill. The official campaign for the State election had already begun and the representative of Mr P. H. Morton (then leader of the Opposition) Mr R. W. Askin, was late for the ceremony because of campaign commitments.

There was a disingenuous tone in Cahill's voice as he spoke: 'Many controversial issues will be raised in the coming election, and to some extent, no doubt, the electorate will be influenced by what is said upon these issues. I am glad to say, however, that the Opera House is purely non-political and I venture to predict that no party will attempt to make an issue of it in the coming election.'

There was a similar tone to the speech by Mr Askin, who is now Sir Robert, Premier of New South Wales. He said 'The time for controversy is over. It only remains for us to work together in a spirit of goodwill and raise the necessary finance to bring this magnificent concept into being. I am sure the people of this State will meet this challenge.'

After his speech Cahill moved to the plinth, put the plaque into place and, when he looked somewhat confused about what to do next, Utzon produced a

The last of the tramshed crashes to the ground to make way for the Opera House.

The tramshed being demolished.

metal bolt which he helped the Premier to screw into place in the centre of the plaque. Intersection grooves on the bolt marked the point from which all measurements would be taken. Cahill then tapped a pin into place to stop the bolt from moving, raised his hand and a police car siren sounded. This was the signal for six men, poised ready with their pneumatic drills, and a bulldozer to go into action preparing the site. The band played 'With a Little Bit of Luck,' and the guests adjourned for afternoon tea. Later, the plaque was taken away and over the years was moved from shed to shed (the surveyors picked their own measuring points) until in 1973 it was brought out again and fixed in the place where it had been laid in 1959, at the foot of the great staircase.

Not much happened in the few weeks after the great official ceremony which was largely a public relations exercise and part of Cahill's State election campaign (which he won). But Cahill, against the advice of both Utzon and the engineers from Arup, wanted Civil and Civic at work on the site as soon as possible. He insisted. By May the contractors were fully engaged in building the podium and they were beginning to feel the pinch, structurally and financially, caused by rushing into the job before they — or anybody else concerned with getting the building to stand up — were ready.

To their horror, Civil and Civic found that the ground at Bennelong Point was not as sturdy as they had expected. Years of dumping from the earliest days of the colony had made it a mish-mash of rubble. They found, after work had started, that not a few but 550 concrete piers would have to be sunk to bedrock to support the podium and the roof shells. They also found that harbour water flowed freely into the lower levels of the foundations, which they had not expected.

The building kept falling behind schedule despite Dusseldorp paying well over the award rates to his workers, who were often on the job 10 hours a day. Ironically, when the successful tenderer was named back in February, Dusseldorp had said he did not expect any problems in construction, despite the unique design of the building. It must have been the most over-confident statement ever made about the building — apart from those which minimised costs and the time it would take to build.

Arup and Partners, which had the contract to provide the working drawings for Stage 1, were still working on them when construction began. In effect Civil and Civic were, in many parts of that podium, building something that was still in the design stage. Many problems were to be overcome before the podium was eventually completed in February, 1963 — more than two years behind schedule and at almost double the estimated cost — $5.1 million.

Despite the troubles into which Civil and Civic were running on the site, Sydney was already planning to open its Opera House, on Australia Day 1963, to celebrate the nation's 175th anniversary. Nobody was more enthusiastic than Cahill.

But he was not to see the prize for all his efforts in pushing the reluctant designers, engineers and builders.

In February, when he signed the contracts for Stage 1, Cahill had said: 'I've watched brick by brick being taken from the old tram shed that was here, and I'm going to watch brick by brick of the Opera House go up.'

But a gastric ulcer which had been giving him increasing trouble robbed him of fulfilling that prophesy. He collapsed in Parliament House during a caucus meeting, was driven to Sydney Hospital next door in his official car and he died from complications caused by the ulcer on October 22.

Bitterness, Tragedy in the Early 60's

With the ever-present worry of finance still hanging heavily on the State Government it was decided early in 1960 to revive the mammoth lotteries which had lapsed earlier for want of support. This time, the Government decided, the ticket price would be reduced to $6, which seemed like a sum gamblers were more likely to part with for a chance at $200,000.

And this revival centred attention on another curious aspect of the Opera House project. Was it legal?

Under Cahill the Government had considered this question in Cabinet and decided that the project was all perfectly legal and required no legislation to give it the force of law. Later, minds were changed when the State Crown Solicitor suggested that the Opera House was a public work within the meaning of the Public Works Act and, as such, required parliamentary sanction. The new Premier, Cahill's successor, Heffron, introduced legislation to validate all that had gone before and was yet to come (or at least what was expected to come), on March 22, 1960.

What the Bill did was to validate the design competition and the award of first prize to Utzon, the beginning of construction and the contracts already signed. It also established an official source of money, the Opera House Account, which was to receive revenue from the Opera House lottery, public appeals, State funds and other sources. The Minister for Public Works of the day was designated the man in charge. At that time it was Mr P. N. Ryan. An attached schedule to the Bill said the cost of the Opera House was to be $9.7 million (the figure mentioned a few weeks before by Haviland) and that this was not to be exceeded by any more than 10 per cent. The Bill became an Act of Parliament in April, 1960.

The then Leader of the Opposition, Robin Askin, made a vitriolic attack on the government and declared that the Opera House was more likely to cost $20 million.

Utzon assists Premier Cahill in the setting of the plaque at the ceremony to mark the start of construction.

In one of those ironies that have become characteristic of the Opera House story, Heffron replied: 'I do not think anybody in their right senses would say it will cost up to £10 million ($20 million). This is ludicrous and absurd. You might as well say it will cost £50 million ($100 million).' Which was the sum arrived at as the official final cost.

Civil and Civic were pushing ahead with the podium, working from drawings provided under contract by Arup and Partners, which had a team working in London providing working drawings. As fast as the London team produced a new drawing it was snapped up by Civil and Civic. Animosity was building between Civil and Civic and the design-engineering team. The contractor was beginning to think his claims for extra expenses Civil and Civic had to bear were not being fairly met — and this was later set down in a report on the construction of the podium.

For example, Civil and Civic had to use special percussion drills on the erratic rubble on the site instead of normal drills. It had had to send divers down inside the steel formwork for the concrete piers to pump them out before concrete could be poured. Special cofferdams had to be used to prevent seepage into much of the concrete work deep inside the podium. A stormwater channel and underwater powerlines had to be moved. The foundations of an old vehicular ferry that was used before Sydney Harbour Bridge was opened had to be blasted out of the water.

Add to these problems the frustrating waiting for working drawings that Arup and Partners were churning out as fast as they could, and it becomes fairly easy to understand the irritation felt by Civil and Civic. All this, of course, was a legacy of the insistence on rushing into construction without sufficient planning.

But by the middle of 1960 it was possible to discern what was going on at Bennelong Point. With a little imagination it was possible to visualise the complex of rooms and passageways that would form the inside of the podium, to place the two auditoria shells on top of this and get an idea of the size and shape of the Opera House.

As bitterness grew on the construction site, the most tragic chapter in the Opera House story was unfolding — as a result of the unique system of financing the project.

Basil Thorne, a commercial traveller, held the winning ticket in the Opera House lottery drawn on June 1, 1960. His good fortune was duly reported in the Sydney media and it took the attention of Stephen Leslie Bradley, a sometime confidence man. Bradley set up what became Australia's first recorded kidnapping. He posed as a private detective and visited the Thorne's home to get the lay of the land. On the morning of July 7, the Thorne's son, Graeme, aged 8, disappeared on his way to school. Later, Bradley phoned the Thornes and demanded $50,000. But he had no plans for returning the boy to his parents after receiving the ransom, for almost

Work pushes ahead on the podium.

Excavation and formwork have begun and extension of Bennelong Point over the eastern side of the Harbour is under way.

Ferry commuters parking their cars at Kirribilli on the north side of the Harbour could watch the podium rising on Bennelong Point.

as soon as he had taken Graeme, he killed him by strangling and bashing him.

Graeme's body was found on a vacant lot in suburban Sydney a month later. Bradley fled the country on a ship and was eventually arrested in Ceylon. Detectives had discovered he was living in a fashionable suburb and owned two cars but was working in a poker machine factory on a weekly wage of $36. Bradley was returned to Australia and in 1961 was convicted of murder and sentenced to life imprisonment. He died in Goulburn Jail.

There was plenty of talk about an opening on Australia Day 1963, until August of 1960 when Haviland put a brake on that sort of runaway enthusiasm which had not been checked by any announcements of the delays and difficulties being encountered by Civil and Civic.

'A lot of people do not realise that plans to open the Opera House in January 1963 have been abandoned as the building can't be completed by that time,' Haviland said. 'It will not be opened until early 1964.'

Work progressed and the Government gave consideration to the running of the Opera House after it was opened. In February 1961 it introduced legislation to establish the governing body, the Sydney Opera House Trust — with the Premier as president and a number of trustees nominated by the president.

A few weeks later the Government announced that a $3.4 million contract for the construction and installation of stage machinery had been let to the Austrian firm, Wagner Biro, a world leader in the field.

On April 11, 1961, the Sydney Opera House Trust had its first meeting and assumed responsibility for administration, control, management and maintenance of the Opera House and its site. In a masterful piece of understatement, Heffron announced at that first meeting that the final cost of the Opera House would shock the Government and the public.

Normal rises in costs would take the cost to $13 million from the previous estimate of $9.6 million. And this would not be a final figure, said Professor Ashworth, chairman of the technical panel. It had taken one year for the estimate to reach the figure which Heffron had labelled as ludicrous during debate on the Opera House Bill.

The bitter story of the podium construction continued for another two years. Its bitterness is illustrated by a report to the technical panel from one of the consulting engineers on the site:

'The architect and the consulting engineers are very dissatisfied with the contractor's workmanship, leadership and supervision. The contractor is critical of the way his claims have been dealt with by the consulting engineers and feels he is not being reimbursed sufficiently for tasks he is asked to perform.'

Utzon made several visits to Australia, breaking his work on the roofs in Denmark and London,

during this time. One such visit came after he was summoned by the State Government, in August 1962. The press said he had come prepared to answer charges that his creation would cost $30 million.

Utzon said: 'The talks are quite normal. They are to discuss the beginning of the second stage.'

Utzon and Arup, who had come with him, went into huddles with the technical panel and the Government, for a thorough examination of the structure and its costs.

At the end of a long meeting Heffron announced that the Opera House would now cost $25 million and work would be finished by the end of 1965. This was a complete cost, he said, and one based on the most accurate assessments possible at the time. It included calculations based on Utzon's final proposals for the complex roof structure — that of a spherical geometry and prefabricated.

Utzon at the time said he and his team would provide Sydney with a perfect Opera House — regardless of cost. He also said he would soon return to Sydney to set up a permanent base.

As work was drawing to a slow and bitter close on the first stage of the Opera House and the continuing row over rising costs was running hot, the Government announced that it had let the contract for the construction of Stage 2, the roof vaults, to M. R. Hornibrook (NSW) Pty Ltd — now a subsidiary of Britain's Wood Hall. The terms of the contract were that the contractor would get a flat fee for management of $150,000 and the Government would meet the cost of site labour and plant and materials. The flat fee was later increased because of the increase in Hornibrook's workload. Estimated time of completion for Stage 2 was January 1965 and total cost was estimated at $3.6 million.

The Roofs

The podium is the stomach of the Opera House; the roof sails are its spirit. Utzon came to Australia to live and supervise closely and minutely their construction. Until 1963 he had worked and lived in Denmark and made many visits to Australia but for the roof vaults he needed to be on the spot.

The Hornibrook Group had been invited to contract for the job and moved on to Bennelong Point in March, 1963, a few weeks after Utzon had come to Australia to live. The group's job was to give life to Utzon's dream, to realise the thousands of hours of work that had gone into planning the roofs and to cross some more technical thresholds with Utzon and Arup.

Utzon had been wrestling with the structure of his gracefully curved, almost impossibly shaped roof system almost since he won the design competition. He had made his first contact with Arup and Partners as early as 1957 and together they had struggled to find a way to make the Utzon vision work — while Cahill pressed ahead with his project, merely assuming that they would find a way. Incredibly, nobody had any idea of whether the roofs could be built and then made to stay there, when work began on the podium. It was unheard of in construction and, probably, never will happen again.

The first freehand sketches that Utzon submitted in the design competition showed a gracefully curving roof system which rose fairly sharply from the podium but then flattened out to form a much less acute rise. The vision was one of a fairly elongated shell group. But there was virtually no definition to the shape — engineers could not define it in geometric terms. This had to be done first so that there was some sort of system whereby the various stresses and forces operating on the structure could be calculated.

Utzon saw the shells being cast in concrete, in situ. The idea was that a massive scaffolding framework would be built and from this the concrete would be poured to form a contiguous shell. When the scaffolding was removed the concrete shell would remain, supporting itself, much as a dome bears all its own weight, transferring the stress down through its shape to the ground. This was the scheme on which most of the early work was done.

Utzon planned a system of two thin concrete shells each about nine inches thick on either side of a system of concrete beams, thus making a unified shell roof about four feet thick. This was because a single shell system, without the support of ribbing or beams, could not carry its weight in the shape Utzon had envisaged. He had been prepared at the earliest stages to modify his shape but not to the extent that would have been required to enable this system of construction.

Originally the design was looked at as being free form, but then the engineers developed a series of parabaloids and then ellipsoids on which to work. These gave geometric regularity to the curving surfaces of the roofs. But before these, much work was done with computers and a specially invented system of plotting in an attempt to produce working drawings for the roof shapes. With the ellipsoids the engineers would have met some of Utzon's requirements, notably the one that the roof shells should have a plane base, which would then be tipped up to rise at an angle from the podium.

Two models were built, one to test the stresses and various forces at work on the shells within the structure and the other to test the effects of Sydney Harbour's winds on the structure. The tests, carried out at Southampton University, in Britain, showed that the structure was likely to resist wind forces of up to 90 mph but that there was some bending, which had been detected in electronic measurements in the wind tunnel tests. Similarly, bending was measured in the structural test model, to which had been attached over a thousand weights designed to correspond with the various forces at work on the structure. But in this development each roof system was a series of interconnected shells. It became apparent to some engineers that, while some of the shells over both

Intricate stress tests were made on early models of the roofs.

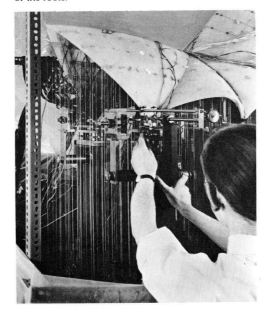

roof systems would be very stable, others would not.

They saw the Opera House being like a house of cards: when one shell fell after too much movement in, say, a freak gale, some of the others would go too. What they wanted was a system whereby each shell could be made to stand stable and independent of its neighbour. And Utzon's requirement that each shell should be tilted so that it rested only on two points made this difficult, to say the least.

In addition to this engineering problem there were other objections to the system which was being developed. Utzon, who had created a most striking shape in his Opera House, feared that the surface texture of concrete cast in situ would look too flat, bland and boring on the inside of the building. (The tiles would take care of the texture outside.) And then there was cost. It was apparent early in the 1960s that the building was going to cost a lot more than Sydney had dreamed of — especially if this massive scaffolding framework was to be built, the concrete carted up into it and poured. The cost would have been prohibitive, even for the Sydney Opera House.

Utzon and Arup began to look at alternative forms of construction. Utzon, while a great visionary designer, is also a practical man, interested in the economies provided by prefabrication. He has been a champion of prefabrication and industrialised building (factory manufacture of components which are assembled on site).

In this search for an alternative to the great grid of scaffolding and formwork a system was examined which involved the use of giant concrete ribs which would be placed so close together they would support the outside skin of tiles. This idea appealed to Utzon because it meant at least a step towards prefabricating the Opera House roofs — all the ribs would have to be cast on the ground then raised into position to form the vaults. But the shape of the roofs was still being developed on the plan for a series of ellipsoids, which is an irregular shape.

Few sections of an ellipsoid are repeated elsewhere in the ellipsoid and this meant that almost every component of the roof section would have to be cast from its own unique mould. Again, cost was the stumbling block.

It was back to the drawing boards. Again thousands of computer calculations had to be scrapped. Another approach had to be taken. Exhausted engineers had to refire themselves and approach the problem with new zest after yet another in a long series of disappointments lasting more than three years.

It was the sort of thing that led Ove Arup to say about that time: 'Speaking for us, I would say we are quite crazy to take this job. I'm not complaining. I'm just saying that's how it is. I never realised it would be so hard. I don't know of any other firm in the world which would have put up with what we have had to put up with. It's taken two or three years off my life.'

Utzon has among his many attributes a talent with geometry. And it was his knowledge of geometry and the characteristic Utzon flair with it that led to the solution to the problem of making the roofs stand up. It had been said that the idea came to Utzon while he was peeling an orange but he says it evolved from his close observation of the shipyards near his home (his father was a top naval architect) and their work with curved shapes. In a phone call to Arup in London Utzon suggested that perhaps a sphere was the shape needed. Utzon worked fast. The sphere provided something that Utzon felt was at last going to work, work well and work economically. That its completely regular shape suggested the opportunity to cast all the components from relatively few moulds further fired his enthusiasm because it was a fine illustration of the advantages of prefabrication.

Overnight Utzon had the local shipyard build a wooden model of a sphere for him, which showed how the various segments could be cut from it to produce all the components required for the Opera House roof system. Arup went to Denmark to see the models and was enthusiastic.

Not so enthusiastic were the staff of Arup and Partners who, by late 1961, had spent more than three years and more than 100,000 man hours on calculations, tests and drawings on possible methods of building the roof. Here was yet another. But to Utzon it meant not only the closest means technically possible for erecting his roofs but it also meant that if the spherical geometry and prefabricated rib system could be made to stand up it would come very close to achieving the interesting look he was seeking for the interior surfaces of the vaults. It would provide a massive ribbed surface giving an effect of contrasting light and shade.

It meant a major change from the design that was being developed from the original sketches and the NSW Government, which had been financing this development, had to be told. Not only was it a massive structural and technical breakthrough but it meant a radical change in the external appearance of the Opera House. Utzon's early sketches had shown a pattern sharply rising and slowly flattening curves housing the auditoria. Now the shells would rise in a completely regular arc. Sydney had to approve the structural change and had to be satisfied with the aesthetics it presented.

In March 1962 Utzon came to Sydney with Jack Zunz, the Arup engineer appointed to take charge of the Opera House project. At a meeting of the technical panel in Sydney the designer and engineer explained the changes that were in mind. They pointed out problems, such as achieving sufficient volumes inside the halls with the space restrictions imposed by the spherical shape, but they also pointed out that it seemed the most promising system yet looked at for actually getting the roofs built. (Work on the podium at this stage was becoming well advanced. A solution to the problem of the roofs was becoming an ever more pressing need.)

They suggested to the technical panel that a sphere with a radius of 246 feet would provide the volumes required in the hall for acoustical purposes; some agonising work on the seating arrangements would lead to a way of fitting enough people inside. They presented a successor to the Red Book, known as the Yellow Book, to explain the geometry of the new scheme. Utzon explained the advantages of the rib roof system and its prefabrication from the parts of this 246 feet radius sphere, pointing out that it would be not only fast, but relatively inexpensive. The new scheme won the approval of the technical panel and later the Minister for Public Works, Ryan, who had been designated the constructing authority in the Opera House Act, gave the go-ahead officially.

This meant many more hours of calculations, drawings and tests. The new roofs had to be made to stand up, for example. An old problem. The fears of one roof shell bringing down the rest were raised again.

What eventuated was the system that now keeps the Opera House roof sails in place on Bennelong Point and allows audiences to sit comfortably within the building without worrying about the possibility of a high wind bringing them down.

There are three shell systems — one over the restaurant, one over the Opera Theatre and one over the Concert Hall. Each of the systems is a series of shells which are interconnected but which stand independently. Each of the vaults is an individually stable structure.

Taking the Concert Hall roof (which is identical to that over the Opera Theatre, but larger) the system works this way:

Each of the four shells are numbered, A1 nearest the main steps and A4 nearest the Harbour. The first two shells, A1 and A2, stand back to back, each on its own two legs. Between them are side shells which fill in the space between the bases of the two main shells. The side shells themselves are supported by a massive pillar or leg of their own. Together A1, A2 and the side shells form a completely integrated structure which stands on six legs. The next shell towards the Harbour is A3. It appears to rise out of the mouth of A2. But on close inspection a small 'louvre' shell can be seen rising backwards into the mouth of A2. Shell A3 and the 'louvre' shell are back to back and connected with a side shell. Each rests on its own pair of legs. Thus the structure which is, in essence, shell A3, rests on four legs and is independent of the rest of the roof system. A similar structure makes A4 stand up independently on its own four legs. The system is repeated on a smaller scale for the Opera Theatre roof. The shells over the Bennelong Restaurant are virtually a repetition of the structure which makes A1 and A2 stand up.

Once Ryan had given his official approval to the change in plans Utzon and Arup began discussions with the Hornibrook Group, which they wanted to build their shells.

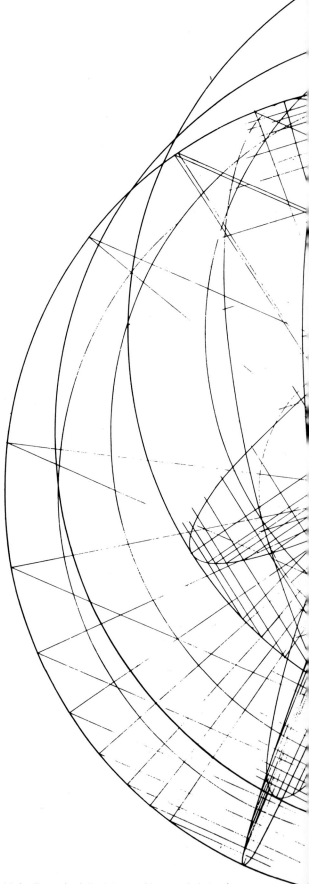

Utzon's geometry on the spherical shape which finally resolved the design problems with the roofs.

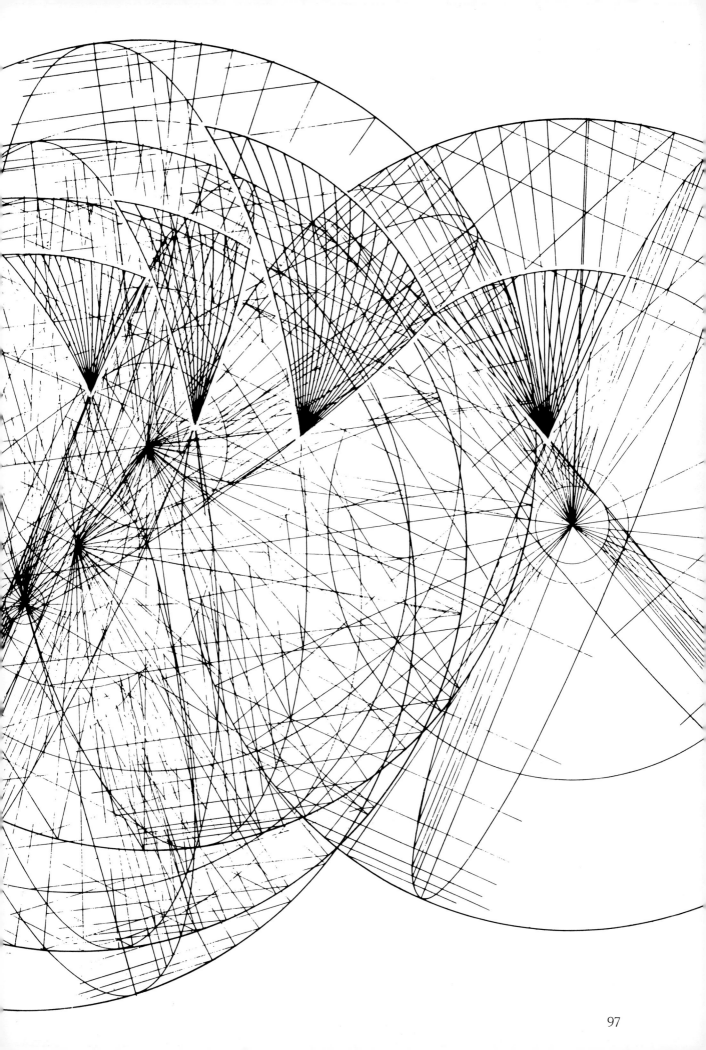

The Hornibrook Group had grown from a small Queensland business to one of Australia's biggest construction contractors and they had been recommended to the architects and engineers by Arup and Partners' Australian representatives of the time, MacDonald, Wagner and Priddle. The company was awarded the contract in October 1962 but earlier, almost immediately after Ryan's approval had been given to the project, Corbet Gore, who was to be Hornibrook's project manager, began work.

With another engineer he began to investigate the problems that would be posed for the builders of this complex and intricate structure that was still being designed and drawn in the London office of Arup and Partners. In the United States he investigated the latest developments in epoxy resin glues and became convinced that this would be a satisfactory method of joining the rib segments together, one on top of the other, as they rose from the podium into the air. This glue, a form of the common household Araldite, was so strong that in some tests the concrete broke apart before the glue gave way at a join. The glue was to be assisted by post stressing of the rib segments with steel cable.

Gore also went to France where, he had been told by Arup and Partners, he would see the only type of construction crane that would be suitable for this unique job. He bought three at $100,000 each — 250 feet high, with an operating radius of 164 feet, and capable of lifting up to 20 tons. And all the time work was progressing in the London office of Arup and Partners, with the computers computing and the designers designing and the plotters plotting.

A year after Utzon and Zunz had explained the design changes to the technical committee in Sydney, Hornibrook's moved on to the site — still with much of the engineering work on the roofs to be done.

Their arrival was heralded with a bang. The Sydney Daily Mirror of the day declared: 'A major blunder revealed yesterday in the construction of the Sydney Opera House will add a fortune to its cost. Twenty reinforced concrete columns built to carry the roof cannot support the load. This is because the roof design was changed last year, after work on the base of the building had begun.'

It was a graphic example of the major problem besetting the Opera House — that of rushing in before design work was complete.

Ove Arup had some terse comments: 'It is only one of a million troubles. The Opera House is being built on a trial and error basis. If the planners had been given five years to design the building, instead of being rushed into it for political reasons, about $4 million might have been saved on the ultimate cost.'

Utzon had arrived to live in Sydney a few weeks earlier and, when the Hornibrook Group inspected the podium that had been left them by Civil and Civic, they found that it had been built to the specifications laid down when the base was expected to support a thin, and fairly light, concrete shell system. But now the roofs were to be built of much heavier precast concrete ribs. The base just was not

Clear directions are posted on striking signs on the forecourt.

strong enough. The only way around the problem was to strengthen a number of concrete piers that had been sunk down through the base to support the roof. And the only way to get at the piers to do this was to blast them with explosives.

But, as Arup had said, it was one of a million troubles. Not the least of these was the unseasonal amount of rain that fell on Sydney during 1963 and held up work.

The rain turned the Hornibrook testing ground at the suburban Sydney depot into a quagmire. Here they had built a number of moulds to test the moulding and erection of the ribs in segments. But they used conventional scaffolding in these tests.

On the Opera House site Corbet Gore planned to use a device he had helped to invent in Sydney, called an erection arch. It was an ingenious complement to Utzon's spherical geometry. In the technology of the time it would have been normal procedure to erect a vast network of scaffolding from which the erection crews would work. But the cost of this would have been enormous. Utzon's geometry helped solve the problem.

Gore developed a moveable steel structure which could assume the precise shape of the arch of ribs that was being built at the time. For instance, it could move from a small arch of ribs to the biggest by careful telescoping of its steel grid. Thus, one scaffolding structure which could telescope up to the size of the biggest pair of ribs took the place of a massive scaffolding network covering the whole construction site.

Two scale models were built and tested.

Except when one of them collapsed, the four erection arches employed on the site were remarkably successful. Not so successful was the first major piece of construction work on Stage 2 at Bennelong Point. The Hornibrook Group chose to begin work on the roofs on the giant leg that was to support the side shells between A1 and A2, on the western side of the Concert Hall entrance foyer. They decided, largely as an experiment, to cast it in situ. It was in places three inches out of place when completed but it was eventually decided not to pull it down and start again. The correction was made later when the shell section was added but today it is still possible to see the error when the arch is looked at against the first main rib next to it. This was a foretaste of survey problems that were yet to come.

Utzon designed each set of shells to straddle axes that converged at a point near the base of what are now the main steps. This was to have been the major survey point during construction but when surveyors came to check the lay of the land before work started they found that this point was not going to be suitable: their sightline would be obstructed by workmen or by the rising building itself. They chose their own from which they could check whether each rib was in its correct position in space as specified by the designers.

Much midnight oil was burned by the surveyors checking their readings to determine just where and

The roof shells begin to rise from the podium, 1964.

Under these trees the Government wanted to build a car park, the builders' labourers refused.

by how many inches each rib had to be moved after it was completed so that its position conformed with that in the plans. (This was done by jacking the completed rib into position.) Later, much of this routine mathematical work was obviated when one of the young surveying team developed a computer system, which utilised the computer of the Australian General Electric Company. Survey readings were programmed and the corrections computed and returned to the site within a couple of hours. This speeded up the work.

But the most ingenious use of computers on the sitework came as a solution to one of the most exasperating problems which occurred during Stage 2 construction. This came when the builders began to attach the tile lids to the rib shells.

The lids, a chevron of concrete into which the tiles had been set on the ground, were to be hoisted on to the rib superstructure and fixed there by bolts and brackets which had been placed earlier.

The problem was encountered during the first full-scale test of the system that had been devised for fixing the tiles — in August 1965. The brackets on the lowermost lids fitted perfectly with the bolts in their corresponding ribs. But as the structure rose higher up the rib the farther out of place were the bolts and the brackets.

All the lids which had been cast might have had to have been scrapped. But the alternative to this seemed much cheaper — that was to devise a way to make the brackets and the bolts come together. The Australian General Electric computer was called into action again, the 2000-odd brackets that had already been fabricated were smelted down and the 4000-odd yet to be made were redesigned.

The builders set about finding out precisely where, in that vast superstructure, each bracket on each lid should be in order to engage the bolt that had been built for it on the rib. Then, in what must have been the most maddening task in Stage 2, the surveyors set about surveying every bolt on every rib. This information was programmed and the computer gave a precise position of every bolt. From this the distance between where each bolt actually was and where it should have been was calculated. This gave the builders the information from which they redesigned the brackets and a number of packing pieces so that each tile lid could be made to connect perfectly with its rib bolt. Each of the new brackets and packing pieces was entered on a computer programme so that for each tile lid the computer could tell the builders precisely what design of bracket and how many of what type of packing pieces were needed to form a perfect marriage between tile lid and roof rib.

All this was not resolved effectively enough for tiling to begin until early in 1966, six months late, and the new system cost an extra $300,000.

A year later, on January 17, 1967, the last of the 2194 rib segments was raised into position on the crown of shell A4, over what was to become the harbourside foyer of the Concert Hall.

The roof ribs begin their radial rise. Casting moulds for the ribs are in the foreground.

Workmen on the erection arch await the arrival of another rib segment being hoisted into position in its special cradle.

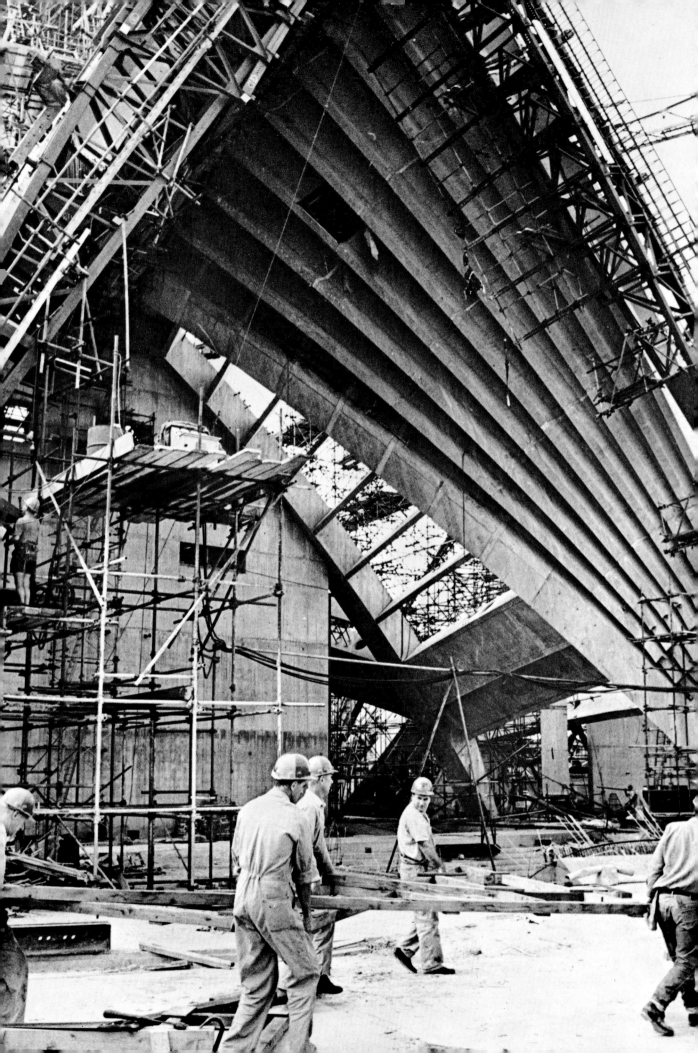

A dogman rides a roof rib segment into position as other workers wait on the erection arch to fix it in place with glue.

The final shape of the Opera House was beginning to appear as the roof ribs were fixed into the giant concrete web.
Work goes on in what would become the entrance foyer of the Concert Hall.

One of the giant arches between what was to become the shells of the Concert Hall.

The ingenious erection arch which telescoped and moved to fit the shape of each individual roof rib as it was being built.

What was to become the vehicle concourse made a fine carpark for workers during construction.

By 1966 Sydney's ferry commuters had a very good idea of what the Opera House was going to look like when finished.

Other Problems in Stage 2

The sculptural aspects of the structure presented by far the most spectacular problems during the early 1960s — but Stage 2 had its other problems. There was the unusual amount of rain which so often interrupted work in 1967 and so many industrial disputes that one newspaper estimated there had been one stoppage a day every day in the first 15 months of Stage 2 work, a loss of 57,000 man hours, 4000 of them in a fight for extra lavatories for the workers.

Relationships between the people working on the site became strained many times and the relationship between Utzon and the Government had begun to deteriorate. Costs continued to rise and in June 1964 the Government issued another revised estimate which gave the price of the Opera House as $34.8 million and the completion date was put back to 1967.

Ryan said he had asked Utzon to examine all possible economies which might cut the costs without sacrifice to the aesthetics of the building.

He added in his announcement of the new estimate: 'This is not the final estimate.'

Utzon countered this with: 'We are doing it as inexpensively as we can.'

There was no way to reduce the cost without sacrificing the quality of the building, he said.

The public learned that no car park had been planned and Utzon made it fairly clear he didn't want one near his Opera House.

The Government and the builders were getting increasingly anxious for Utzon to produce some drawings for Stage 3, the interiors of the building, but he was insisting on model testing for many of his ideas. There were other problems with the interiors of the building, too. Stage machinery contracts and lighting contracts had been signed back in 1961 and 1962 and by 1964 pieces of valuable equipment were beginning to arrive in Sydney with nowhere to go because of the delays in construction. There were problems with the seating and the acoustics.

Utzon had his own problems, too. When he arrived with his family he planned to build a house at Bayview overlooking Sydney's picturesque Pittwater but the local council rejected his plans because they provided for three separate structures. He rented a house at Palm Beach and one in Paddington and worked from these as well as from a boatshed at Palm Beach and an office on the site. Heffron retired in 1964 and was succeeded by Jack Renshaw as Premier. Renshaw was to lead the Government into a State election on May 1, 1965 and as the campaign built up so did every controversial aspect of the Opera House.

Cost and lack of correct management were the issues Robin Askin (who later changed his name by deed poll to Robert) as Leader of the Opposition concentrated on in his campaign.

Askin said, somewhat prophetically, of the project: 'Sydney may not see the finished article until well into the 1970s. Its astronomical price could then qualify it as the eighth and possibly the most precious wonder of the world.'

Utzon was irritated by the constant exposure of the Opera House as an election issue and especially angered by accusations that his fees were abnormally high (he had earned more than $1 million but he had also spent heavily from his own pocket on the project). Angered, he told reporters he was tired of Sydney's negative attitude towards the cost, the delays and the industrial unrest on the site.

An Election and Utzon's Resignation

At the election on May 1, 1965, New South Wales decided, after a record of 24 years of Labor Government, to change its leadership. The Liberal Party-Country Party coalition won the election and Askin became Premier. More importantly, for Utzon, Davis Hughes became the Minister for Works. Now the Opera House was subjected to renewed pressures similar to those which had harried the project in its earliest days.

The pressures were largely political. Cahill had promised to at least begin building an Opera House in Sydney and he had made great play of it in his election campaign. Askin had promised to finish the Opera House, put some strong management into it and minimise the cost. He too had made great play of this in his election campaign.

Hughes recognised the importance of his portfolio, both to himself and to the Government. He threw himself into the job with missionary zeal. He might have better been called the Minister for the Opera House for this was the project on which he spent most of his time and energy, despite other wide ranging activities of the Public Works Department which required his attention.

He began by poring over the Opera House files, soaking up the facts and figures and finding out about the people involved. His first meetings with Utzon were amicable enough. But this honeymoon was not to last.

Three things became immediately apparent to Hughes as he worked his way through the mass of papers in 12 hour shifts in his office: the lack of planning for a car park was confirmed; it was clear that even the most recently revised estimate of $34.8 million was a long way short of the mark; and while Stage 2 was proceeding, little in the way of working drawings was coming forward for Stage 3.

Rumours began to circulate and there were leaks to the media that the new Government was going to find the real price of the project would be close to $50 million. The papers ran the stories in their usual bold way and, despite their familiarity with the story of rising costs at Bennelong Point, Sydney people continued to react. Hughes remained silent however, waiting until he could issue a firm, new estimate.

Perhaps to divert attention away from the immediate concern of costs, he advised the Government that $2 million should be set aside for planning and construction of a car park for the

Construction on Western Broadwalk.

Opera House. He also thought it wise to advertise the position of general manager of the Opera House, a post which had been advertised in 1961 but an appointment deferred because of the uncertain finishing time of the project. Hughes sought to placate a querulous public by announcing: 'We want the Opera House finished at maximum efficiency.'

The way Hughes saw it as he sifted through the information, acquainting himself with the project, was that it was quite likely the Opera House might never have been finished — or at least have taken another 15 years — had it been allowed to continue on the path it was then following. He was quite shocked to find that there were very few working drawings being made for Stage 3, which was the interiors and the external cladding of the podium. He began to get a real and nagging fear that unless he took some firm and positive action the building would run down to a point where work on it would stop completely for lack of plans. Not only would this be bad in general terms but it would be particularly bad for the new Government which had promised to bring some management expertise to the project.

But, before doing much else he wanted to know the size of the latest cost estimate, and until this was available he was going to hold costs in check. While his aides were still at work on the cost estimate, Hughes announced at the end of July that he had appointed a personal watchdog. This was his first shot fired directly at Utzon. More were to come before Utzon finally succumbed.

R. A. P. Johnson, who had retired as State director of Public Works only a month earlier after 49 years service, was appointed with the official explanation that it was one of a series of stringent measures the Government would take to bring costs into line after 'stunning' increases during the previous year under Labor.

Johnson had retired on a pension of $96 a week and was to receive $28 a day. He was to oversee complicated contracts for the completion of Stage 3, as Davis Hughes' representative on the site.

He explained his job: 'My job will be to keep the minister fully informed on what is happening. We expect fresh problems to arise and my appointment is to ensure full co-ordination of activities. This has got nothing to do with inefficiency. A lot more will be going on at the site and it is most important procedures be laid down to ensure they work together.'

This appointment hurt Utzon deeply, just as it had hurt when Ryan appointed a representative (with less sweeping terms of reference than Johnson). Ryan's move had helped to accelerate the decline of his relationship with Utzon. The architect saw the new move by Hughes as a challenge to his integrity and an implied lack of respect for his work as an architect.

At the end of August, Askin confirmed the staggering rumours about the latest rise in price. He announced that the Government had carried out its own survey of the costs. The Opera House now would cost at least $49.4 million and this was without providing the parking for 1000 cars recommended by Hughes or improvements to the approaches to Bennelong Point. One member of the Legislative Council ventured to suggest that from past experience the figure was more likely to be $100 million but nobody took much notice of this piece of fortune-telling.

The building had by now well and truly passed the point of no return. In fact it was sufficiently advanced for its first party. In October Sir Bernard Heinze, the great Australian conductor, and Lady Heinze were guests of honour at a cocktail party put on in the concrete skeleton by the NSW Opera Company and the Rosenkavalier Group. And a few days later there was another party with wild pop music thundering out of the half-completed roof vaults.

But this party mood was soon to fade. That same month, October, Davis Hughes asked for a detailed timetable of the work Utzon had in hand and when he proposed to complete designs for Stage 3. Hughes also announced that in future there would be no tendering by appointment, that all tendering was to be competitive, and that all decisions on administration would be made by him. This meant that Hughes had made himself personally responsible for spending on the project. Utzon was to answer to him.

These new controls, especially the directive on tendering, were the catalysts which brought to a head the two central issues which led to Utzon's resignation — the plywood acoustic ceilings and the system of advance fee payments.

Hughes' decision that all tendering be competitive put paid to two of Utzon's plans. One of these was a special type of reconstituted granite which he had asked Concrete Industries Monier to develop for him for the external cladding on the podium, with a virtual guarantee of the contract for the job. Under Hughes the job was to be put out to tender — despite recommendations from the technical panel that Utzon should be allowed to proceed as he had planned. This was bad enough for Utzon, but worse was the effect of the directive on his arrangement with Ralph Symonds Ltd, who had been working over the years with the architect to develop a system for the ceilings of both the auditoria at Bennelong Point.

With his great faith in prefabrication — especially after the success of the roof ribs — Utzon wanted many of the most important parts of the Opera House built by prefabrication. This, he reasoned, gave him the opportunity to develop, test and modify sections of the building before they were actually put into place. This was the case with the acoustic ceilings he wanted installed. The ceiling system, he and the acoustic consultants planned, was to take the form of giant cylindrical boxes, lead-lined to insulate them from noise and hot-bonded around sheet aluminium to give them the strength to resist the structural forces that would act on them. He proposed to hoist these into position after they had been perfected on the ground. Installed they would give a sweeping, looping effect to the ceiling and their appearance would be dictated by acoustical needs. Ralph Symonds was the only plywood firm in Australia, probably the world, that had the machinery sophisticated enough to build these cylindrical boxes from one sheet of plywood.

These developments were taking place when Ryan was minister and a short time before the State election Utzon wrote to the minister and explained that he wanted Symonds to build models of the ceiling cylinders for testing. He asked Ryan for permission to go ahead because Ryan had to authorise the expenditure. Implicit in the proposal, which had the backing of the technical panel, was that Symonds would get the contract when the system was perfected. Ryan was put out of office by the election before he was able to reply.

When Hughes took the chair at the Works Department he investigated Utzon's letter, especially in the light of claims made by some other manufacturers that they could do the job just as well by joining sheets of plywood to make the ceiling boxes. While some manufacturers said that the order was likely to be big enough to warrant buying the machinery needed, Utzon said that joins were unacceptable in his ceiling boxes and he reasoned that it would be faster if Symonds were allowed to continue since they had already done some experimental work on the scheme. Hughes asked Arup and Partners to report on the proposals.

Arups had some objections. The boxes would be too heavy, too costly and too hard to put in place. The Hornibrook Group added that they thought it would be very difficult to get the highly finished boxes from the factory to the site and into position without damaging them. And they would also be very difficult to sling from the roof since some of them would weigh up to 10 tons. Utzon received these objections in a report in January 1966 and he dutifully passed them on to Hughes.

Hughes rejected Utzon's proposal and insisted that the ceiling project go to competitive tendering.

Utzon was furious for a number of reasons, not the least that his carefully planned scheme for the ceilings had been virtually rejected. But his anger also highlighted the low to which relations between Utzon and Arups had sunk over the years. He thought that the engineers had torpedoed his plans several times without fully investigating them and then come up with their own solution which was unsatisfactory to Utzon. But by now Arups were directly responsible to the minister, which is contrary to normal practice where consulting engineers are responsible to the architect. But back in 1963 Arups had felt they were carrying too large a work load and asked to be relieved of all consulting work except for civil and structural engineering. Since then all other consulting work had been handled by Utzon, who authorised payment. The arrangement by which Arups reported directly to the minister had been a continuing thorn in Utzon's side.

Utzon, in a pre-resignation news conference.

Davis Hughes. His mission was to put some businesslike administration into the lagging construction project.

Hughes's refusal to allow Utzon to go his own way on the ceilings led to the final blow. Angered by this slight to his independence and integrity Utzon decided to press a claim he had made previously but allowed to languish, for $102,000 — a fee he said was due to him for engineering consultancy work done some years back on the development of stage machinery. The refusal was the catalyst that sent Utzon into action but the chemicals had been at work for some time before.

As part of the Government's new management approach to the Opera House Hughes had decided to tighten up the system whereby Utzon was given monthly advance payments to cover running costs and pay his staff. Hughes warned Utzon that this system would not be allowed to continue unless the architect produced some plans for Stage 3 or at least the evidence that he was working on them.

'No plans, no pay,' was the essence of Hughes' message. That was late in 1965 and by the time the ceilings incident had come to a head the Government had stopped paying Utzon his advances. Both from financial necessity — his staff had to be paid — and from the anger aroused by the rejection of his ceilings scheme Utzon decided to press his claim for $102,000.

Much later, Hughes told the NSW Parliament that an arrangement had been made to pay Utzon during 1966 on the same $20,000 a month basis as had existed before. But in future it would have to be related to his work on Stage 3.

On February 28, 1966, Utzon went to Hughes's office in Macquarie Street. He took with him his Australian assistant, Bill Wheatland. The discussion was pretty short. Utzon asked about his $102,000 and Hughes said the claim was still being investigated and that he would have an answer for the architect at the end of the week. Utzon decided to take no more procrastination. He told Hughes he needed the money and was always being put off by the Minister. Hughes repeated that he would give Utzon an answer by the end of the week.

'I resign,' said Utzon and walked out the door, followed by Wheatland.

Back in his office at Bennelong Point Utzon wrote his letter of resignation:

'In the meeting between yourself and Mr Wheatland and me today, you stated you still would not accept my fee claims for $102,000 for stage techniques which I have requested from you for the past several months, which is completely justified. I was forced to set February 15, 1966, as the final date for receipt of this payment. As you could not at this date, February 28, 1966, satisfy me on this, you have forced me to leave the job. As I explained to you, and you know from meetings and discussions, there has been no collaboration on the most vital items of the job in the last many months from your department's side. This also forces me to leave the job as I see clearly that you do not respect me as an architect. I have therefore today given my staff notice of dismissal. I will notify the consultants and the

Workmen fix the chevron shaped tile lids into position on the roof.

Fixing the tile lids into place was precarious work, often carried out from special bosun chairs.

contractors. I will have cleared my office of my belongings and you will receive my final account before March 14, 1966.'
The letter was hand delivered to Hughes and he accepted it immediately.

That night Hughes made the stunning announcement: 'The Government finds the resignation of Mr Utzon a matter of regret and pays tribute to the whole concept of the Opera House which has gained recognition throughout the world. It is the Government's intention to complete the Opera House ensuring that the spirit of the original conception is fulfilled.'

The response was immediate and emotional. Public support for Utzon swelled into a demonstration on March 3 when more than 1000 people carrying placards marched on Parliament House to demand the architect's reinstatement. They were followed by a squad of 30 policemen who kept an eye out for trouble. There was none — despite the provocative presence outside Parliament House of a small group of building workers demonstrating in favour of the appointment of an Australian architect to succeed Utzon. But there were some top people in the demonstration, including Patrick White, who later won a Nobel Prize for literature. White said the Opera House was the only imaginative thing to have happened to dull Sydney.

The same day, Askin announced to parliament that he would try to bring about a reconciliation between Utzon and Hughes.

Utzon, in the meantime, had vanished. Even the most pugnacious of Sydney's reporters could not track him down for comments. But in London, Ove Arup said of the circumstances leading up to the resignation: 'Mr Utzon has been far too stubborn and unyielding on his part and the Government is insisting on things which make it difficult.'

Resignation had crossed Utzon's mind when things became unbearably difficult early in 1966. Only a few weeks earlier Arup had written to him saying: 'As I see it, if you resign, all is lost.' He warned Utzon that resignation would be a most dangerous thing, even to hint at: 'If you want to use it as a threat, you must be quite sure that it will not be accepted. And can you be so absolutely sure?'

Some of Utzon's strongest supporters, notably the distinguished architect Harry Seidler, who had entered the design competition but had championed the Dane through all his trials, tried to convince Utzon that he should return to the job. White and Seidler were among a group of distinguished people who presented Askin with a 3000-name petition demanding Utzon's reinstatement. Seidler also pointed out that day that the Government would find it difficult to get an Australian architect who was willing to try to step into Utzon's shoes.

The next day Seidler and his colleagues met Utzon and tried to persuade him to return to the project. Later, Utzon conferred with Askin in the Premier's office. Reporters spotted him coming out a side door at 6 pm and after pretending to hide behind a

When Utzon resigned the response was immediate, from architecture students as well as a wide section of the community.

companion Utzon spoke to them. He smiled. 'We had a good and friendly meeting. Today's meeting was a good one and there will be a final meeting on Monday,' he said.

Utzon and two assistants, including Wheatland, met Hughes at the Minister's office on Monday, March 7. Also present were the Director of Public Works, C. J. Humphrey, the Government Architect, E. H. Farmer, and Professor Ashworth (an Utzon champion), then head of the technical panel.

Hughes outlined the Government's plan. Utzon could return if he wished but not as the sole architect in charge. He could, if he wished, be the design architect on a panel of architects the Government would appoint to complete the Opera House. Utzon would no longer be in charge. It was proposed that the panel of architects would be responsible to Farmer and the Minister.

Utzon could not accept these conditions. Back in his office at the site he was angry and depressed when he spoke to reporters.

'It is impossible to think of the suggestion that I should be only the designer with a team controlling the actual building of the Opera House. I have designed every line, every corner, every piece of surface. To kill the Opera House might take a long time. But it is dying and sick on the bed now,' he said.

He added that whoever took over the project could not complete it as he had envisaged and that the Government had forced him out.

Around the world the resignation had aroused the attention, ire and sympathy of many. One Danish industrialist offered Utzon all the plywood he needed, free, to complete the building — if only he would stay on and see his vision through.

Then came a James Bond-style meeting between Utzon and Hughes. It was arranged by President of the Royal Australian Institute of Architects, NSW, R. A. Gilling. Utzon and Wheatland drove to a street corner in North Sydney and waited until they saw Gilling's car pull up. They followed it to a motel in Lane Cove where a room had been booked for the meeting. Hughes arrived and reiterated the plan to have the Opera House completed by a panel of architects, with Utzon in charge of design but not solely running the job. He gave Utzon four days to make up his mind, but the conclusion seemed foregone.

On March 15, Utzon replied in a letter to the Minister that he could not continue under the terms proposed.

He wrote: 'Having regard to my great interest in the project and my earnest desire that the Opera House when completed should be of great beauty and a cause for great pride among all Australians, I am still willing to make my services available should that be the Government's desire.'

But the Government's mind was made up and Utzon gave notice to his staff. The world's architects protested. As hundreds of cables of protest flooded into Sydney the Government — Hughes — turned

The Harbourside Restaurant treats diners to quick snacks and drinks in Sydney's finest alfresco setting.

his attention to putting faces to the panel he had proposed. He wanted Farmer to head it and Farmer received a petition from his own staff, including a signature from a young man named Peter Hall, which said Utzon was the only man for the job.

On April 9, Davis Hughes announced the names of the men who would take Utzon's place: Peter Hall, aged 34, an architect in the Public Works Department would take over the design, Lionel Todd would take charge of contracts and D. S. Littlemore would be supervising architect.

Inauspiciously the board bearing Utzon's name was taken down from the sign of credits in front of the Opera House.

'They can tear down the Opera House for all I care,' he said in Denmark a few days later. 'I have informed the NSW Government that I do not want any longer to have my name associated with the Opera House.'

Utzon presented Hughes with a bill for $480,000 (while there had been much criticism over the size of Utzon's fees, it was later claimed that he was $80,000 in the red over the job because of double tax problems).

Hughes said he would investigate it and Utzon countered he would present the Government with no plans or drawings for Stage 3 until his account had been settled. A compromise was reached and, in the presence of legal advisers from both sides, Hughes handed over a cheque for $150,000 and Utzon handed over his drawings. (Later Utzon issued a writ for the remaining $330,000 but received $46,000 in an out of court settlement.)

On April 5 the crown piece, the final segment, was hoisted into position in the main sail of the major hall. In secrecy, under an assumed name, Utzon and his family left Sydney on a flight to Mexico, the United States and Denmark. He escaped the attention of the media — despite a 24 hour watch on his house by reporters.

Utzon was not to return to Australia. He remained embittered about the problems he had encountered and what he regarded as the lack of confidence in his ability to bring the project to a successful con-clusion. He returned to his practice in Denmark and continued to travel the world, looking at architecture, developing his philosophical approach. A number of times he was contacted by Australian newspapers and television stations and usually his comments were hard and biting about what had been done to the Opera House.

He was invited to attend the official opening by the Queen in 1973 but, despite some mellowing of attitude towards Sydney, he declined the invitation. While he bore no grudge against his successors on the site he regretted that they had not followed through the concept he had always held for the Opera House. This, of course, would have been impossible without Utzon on the site. Much of the concept was still inside his head and had not been committed to paper — at least to paper that he would allow others to see.

The Australian flag was planted to mark the peak. finally in position, of the highest shell.

Access to the peak of each shell is along a narrow catwalk along the centre line.

The New Team Takes Over

Hall has often said that he treated the Opera House as a 'found object.' What he found justified the trepidation he had felt in accepting the appointment as the new design architect. All the problems which had been accumulating and which were to beset Hall burst dramatically into the open a few days before Utzon resigned. There was an awareness of some of the problems the building was headed for but at a routine meeting between officials of the Australian Broadcasting Commission and some members of the Opera House Trust these were put into a staggering perspective.

The meeting had been called to discuss the siting and planning of television cables and some other apparently minor points about ABC use of the Opera House when it opened. It was proceeding according to routine when one of the ABC people, an acoustics engineer named W. J. Mehaffey, blurted out that all the talk going on seemed pointless to him. The Opera House as it was being built would be no good for symphony concerts, he said.

This was quite a statement to make since the ABC and its symphony concerts were to be the major user of the Opera House. Mehaffey pointed out that the main hall would not be able to hold sufficient seats to make symphony concerts an economic proposition for the ABC and nor would it be big enough to achieve the reverberation time required by the Sydney Symphony Orchestra.

He added that the rehearsal room provided for in Utzon's plans was big enough only for an orchestra of about 30 players, and it would not be big enough for the SSO rehearsals. Nor would it be capable of doubling as a recording studio or a broadcasting studio. Driving a final nail, Mehaffey said that harbour noise and the sound of the air conditioning would penetrate into the auditoria.

Understandably his statements staggered those at the meeting. They were probably the spark for the bitter row which followed over the design and use of the major hall, the most public row between the ABC and the Elizabethan Theatre Trust which came to a head later in 1966.

Hall and his new partners walked into the building with little or no detailed information on what was expected of Stage 3. At first they had none of Utzon's drawings. Later they were given 115, but some of these, Hall said, were incomplete. It was a matter of starting from scratch. With public controversy raging over the seating shortfall that had been left by Utzon in the major auditorium, Hall left for a tour abroad during which he would study concert halls and opera theatres and discuss with the various consultants to the Opera House just what work they had done and how they could contribute towards the completion. Though it had been represented (in a personal rather than ex officio role) on the Opera House Trust by Sir Charles Moses, the then general manager, the ABC had never given a complete, detailed list of its requirements in the building. Soon after the Mehaffey revelations the commission, under its present general manager,

Talbot Duckmanton, was asked for such a document. After painstaking research by officers of the ABC, Duckmanton eventually told the new architects what was wanted.

Broadly, the ABC wanted to seat 2800 people; it wanted a stage big enough for a large orchestra, a choir and an organ; it wanted a reverberation time suited perfectly for symphony concerts; and it wanted complete soundproofing of the auditorium it was to use.

These requirements were presented to Hall in June 1966, shortly before the new man took off on his 12 week study tour abroad. When he returned to Australia Hall had looked at scores of foreign concert halls and opera theatres and had concluded that opera and concert were totally incompatible within one auditorium, a view which Talbot Duckmanton had expounded on behalf of the ABC. The Government instructed Hall to investigate the ABC's requirements.

Most of the rest of 1966 was spent by the new architectural panel evaluating the project they had inherited and devising a brief for themselves. They set about finding out just what was wanted — once and for all — inside the Opera House. And they began to think about how it could all be executed.

In September that year Hughes made a bitter attack on Utzon. He was speaking in a debate in the NSW Parliament to an amendment to the Opera House Act authorising increased spending up to a new high of $37.5 million. He said Utzon had made no working drawings or specifications for Stage 3.

'The most glaring example and indeed the most frightening omission is the almost calamitous deficiency in the seating plan for the main hall. Complete chaos and confusion on this aspect have been revealed,' he said.

While all this 'chaos and confusion' was being revealed and studied and worked on to reach some sort of workable conclusion, the row between the ABC and the Elizabethan Theatre Trust, under the nuggety leadership of Dr H. C. Coombs, was shaping up. It was to be a rough and bitter fight.

The ABC on the one hand claimed that the major hall should be used only for symphony concerts and that opera should be relegated to another part of the Opera House complex.

Dr Coombs, a former Governor of the Reserve Bank, argued that the main hall could still be kept for both concerts and opera. If the ABC had its way, Coombs saw, then Sydney would not be able to stage grand opera because the minor hall would not be big enough.

Coombs is a fierce adversary, highly skilled in the guile and cunning that took him from the West Australian goldfields to his present height in the national bureaucracy. (An ex-Governor of the Reserve Bank, he is now a special adviser to Prime Minister Whitlam.) But the ABC wielded a strong weapon — its patronage of the Opera House, which ultimately would decide the economic viability of the project.

Peter Hall surveyed the project he was to complete after Utzon's resignation.

Davis Hughes shows Opera House Trust chairman Sir Philip Baxter over the site.

Peter Hall and Lionel Todd ponder some of the problems they inherited after Utzon's resignation.

The argument raged. In January 1967, after months of work, especially with the American theatre consultant Ben Schlanger, the architectural panel came out with its first 'Review of Program.' It virtually spelt the end for Dr Coombs's argument.

The architects said:

The major hall should be made into a concert hall satisfying the ABC's criteria. It should no longer try to be a multi-purpose hall. To gain the floor area needed for the increased seating and the volume needed to produce a reverberation time of about two seconds the proscenium arch and the stage tower should be removed, allowing the ceiling to sweep uninterrupted from one end of the hall to the other.

To use the major hall as a concert hall was reasonable only if a satisfactory alternative theatre could be offered for opera and ballet. The minor hall at 1100 seats with its tiny orchestra pit, would not do. Its capacity could, however, be increased to 1500 by the addition of galleries and an enlargement of the pit to accommodate around 80 musicians.

The advantages of having a large auditorium for concerts and a reasonably sized separate theatre for opera make this alteration seem sensible. It was pointed out that a convertible theatre in the main hall (one that could be converted from opera to concerts and back again fairly quickly) was possible but that it would require extensive, expensive new stage machinery.

Dr Coombs did not give up hope and through February 1967 there was a series of meetings between the ABC, the Elizabethan Theatre Trust, the architects and the State Government over how the problem of the halls should be resolved. Coombs put some pretty tough arguments but the ABC stood its ground. Then the Opera House Trust, whose function really was the management of the building when completed, came down on Dr Coombs's side. But to no avail.

In the meantime Utzon had said in an interview that he could design an interior that would suit everybody and he offered to return to Australia if the Government would have him. It would not. About the same time there were more calls to rename the Opera House so that the title would more adequately reflect the diversity of activities that were planned for the building. But Hughes stood firm on that. The building had been named by Act of Parliament and Sydney Opera House it would remain. In the midst of this argument, Hughes broke his own dictum on Opera House contracts. Rather than call tenders for Stage 3 he appointed Hornibrook as the builder who would complete the Opera House. There was no timetable laid down in the contract, but nobody seemed to be irritated by this reversal of his own orders.

Work went on at Bennelong Point, and at the beginning of 1967 the last segment of the roof was placed into position. Sir Eugene Goossens, who had fathered the project 20 years earlier, died in London.

The arguments about the use of the two halls were finally laid to rest on March 21, 1967. The

Dr H. C. Coombs.

Premier announced that the State Cabinet, acting on advice from Hughes, had decided to adopt the plans of the architectural panel. The main hall would be reserved for concerts and the minor hall would be reworked as an opera theatre. What the Government had accepted in fact was the preliminary plan for what now appears inside the Opera House, but there was more to come as the plans and work evolved.

In June, work began to dismantle the stage tower and proscenium arch that had been erected inside the main hall. The stage that had been built was concreted over for acoustical improvement. The fact that there would be no proscenium arch in the hall meant that the acoustic envelope inside the hall would be that much larger — enough to provide the reverberation time required by the ABC. Most of the stage machinery dismantled was scrapped because it was of no use to either hall in the new plan.

Work on the rest of the building however had slowed to a crawl. The Government explained this as a part of the transition between Stages 2 and 3. But others said, more correctly, that there was a lack of plans.

The new architects were not going to make the mistakes that had been made earlier with the building. They wanted complete designs before work began. And they were hard into the design problems that Stage 3 presented. Apart from the paving and cladding of the exterior it was to be all their own work and the plans they were working on were to be final.

They were working, somewhat hopelessly, towards a completion date of 1970. But while Peter Hall was at work at the drawing board the only work going on at the Opera House was the completion of the broadwalk and walls, all that was left of construction to Utzon's design. The contractors now were waiting on Hall's designs.

Two years after taking over, the new design team presented the first plans to the Government for approval (it was to be another six months before complete, detailed plans and estimates were handed to the Government). The Government had planned for 1970 completion and as they worked it became increasingly obvious to the architects that they would be unable to meet this deadline. Their fears were confirmed by a report from the management consultants, PA, who had been called in by Hall as project planners, with the task of co-ordinating the construction program. They reported to Hall, and Hall reported to the Government that the project would not be completed for seven years (that was in 1968) and it would cost $100 million. This was probably the first realistic piece of forward estimating that was made of the Opera House cost and timetable. The official estimate of the cost at that time had climbed to $85 million.

It was not until June 1969 that the snail-pace of work at Bennelong Point picked up noticeably. Hall's plans were now approved by the State Government and work was beginning on implementing them. Much of the activity was in pulling down pieces of

Geometry of raw concrete and ceramic tiles.

the structure that were no longer required. By concreting over the stage and removing the tower and proscenium arch in the main auditorium, Hall was able to achieve additional facilities.

What is now the rehearsal-recording hall was a part of the stage well for the Concert Hall.

What is now the Music Room was also made possible by the major change on use of the two big halls.

Construction now was on the final form of the interior — that which is seen at Bennelong Point today. But industrial problems were again besetting the project. Building slowed down again, notably in the middle of 1970 when a strike by builders' labourers cost the project 48,000 man hours. But the interiors nevertheless were beginning to take shape and Hall was at work on other details — the design of the seats, for example, and the colour schemes for all the auditoria. Work had begun on the massive glass walls.

Most of the major problems were well on the way to solution. But one still remained: The car park.

It is quite certain that Utzon virtually ignored the car park problem because, for one thing, it was so far away when he was at work on the building and, for another, he did not want splashes of glinting Duco and chrome spoiling the majestic appearance of the Opera House. He would have favoured the idea of a car park underground, beneath the Botanical Gardens. This was the plan that was eventually put forward.

But militant building workers, led by environmental campaigner Jack Mundey, would not work on it, they said, because to dig beneath the gardens would destroy several fine old Moreton Bay fig trees. The time had come to cease destruction of the environment. They placed a 'green ban' on the project and, apparently, laid it to rest.

But by 1970 there was an air of excitement in Sydney about the building that had become so familiar. It began to look as if it really would, finally, be opened and people would actually sing inside it. The Government that year set a target opening date of March 1973. They were getting closer. There was something tangible about the Opera House that had been almost mystical for so long. People were beginning to talk in vaguely realistic terms about what sort of performances would be held there.

A year later, in September 1971, the Government appointed a deputy general manager, Frank Barnes, who was to succeed the then manager, Stuart Bacon. Much thought was being given to the running of the Opera House as a going concern. Industrial problems were still slowing down work on the project but it was still growing and looking more and more like an opera house and performing arts complex.

Work had progressed well enough by the beginning of 1972 for the Government to appoint a committee to organise an opening ceremony. Sydney's superman of the super-spectacle, public relations man Sir Asher Joel was to take charge of the programme, now finally scheduled for October of the following year. Sir Asher, whose past credits

The Concert Hall foyer, near the entrances to private boxes.

Looking down the eastern foyer of the Concert Hall from the Harbourside foyer. Entrances to seats are off to the right of this area.

A thick, tinted, custom cut glass plate goes into position.

The glass wall-roof over the Opera Theatre's Harbourside foyer.
The steel net, ingeniously designed to carry the glass in the prize-winning glass walls of the Opera House.

One of the first performances in the Opera House, a lunchtime play for construction workers.

A glittering crowd for a charity premiere of the Australian Ballet's film of Don Quixote, a few months before the official opening.

included organising the 1970 Captain Cook Bi-Centenary celebrations in Sydney, set about his crowning achievement. It's been said that only a coronation would top the spectacle he organised on Bennelong Point and around it on October 20, 1973.

In June 1972 the magnificent Coburn tapestries arrived from France and were taken to the Opera House. In July Hughes stepped into a possible dispute over the Music Room-Cinema. He called for a halt to work on that area of the building until the dispute was settled. Peter Hall had proposed to build the auditorium purely as a cinema and the chamber music fans were angry. They had their way and work resumed on the auditorium as a dual purpose hall in October. John Olsen was commissioned to paint his giant mural for the Concert Hall foyer in August. Then in October Sydney entrepreneurs announced that they would be presenting a series of Sunday night popular music programmes with international celebrities as stars — the Opera House was to be for popular taste as well as the finer forms of the performing arts.

Sir Asher Joel was thrilling the Sydney public with tit-bits of his plans for a super-colossal opening ceremony with Her Majesty the Queen. And in December the Premier announced that Hughes would be resigning from the Government to take up a position as the New South Wales Government's Agent General in London. Hughes made the last of his twice-weekly inspections of Bennelong Point on December 7. Claims over who and what were the first performers in the Opera House will be disputed for years and never settled. There was a play in the concrete shell one lunchtime as early as 1967. And there had been parties and fashion parades.

But the first real performance by a symphony orchestra came on December 17, 1972. Sir Bernard Heinze led the Sydney Symphony Orchestra in a concert designed to test and fine-tune the acoustics of the Concert Hall. The Governor of NSW, Sir Roden Cutler, invited guests, and 2700 construction workers who had toiled on the building, turned up for the concert.

Frank Barnes took over from the retiring Stuart Bacon in January 1973 and a month later Utzon indicated he would like to be present at the opening if invited (he later turned down his invitation because as a guest of the Government at the opening he would be unable to honestly answer media questions about what he thought of the final shape of the Opera House).

Barnes announced in March that the Opera House management would also be an entrepreneur and would keep the Concert Hall in use all year, when the ABC was not using it. In making the announcement he pointed out (and the Sydney Press had a field day with this) that the Opera House would cost around $3 million a year to run and the State Government would have to find $2 million a year to subsidise this. In order to raise the remaining $1 million a year it would be necessary to have all the halls fully utilised all the time, he said.

Construction in some degree will always be going on at the Opera House. But it is generally regarded that the dismantling of the three giant tower cranes which had for so long dominated the site at Bennelong Point signified the end of the building program. They came down in April and the same month the architects moved from their little white huts on Bennelong Point to more comfortable offices in the city.

Also in April the Government announced that the Opera House had cost, to that stage, $86 million. And it released a new estimate of the final cost — $99.5 million.

With the end of major construction came the handing over ceremony. The new Minister for Public Works, Mr Punch, handed over the Opera House officially to the Minister for Cultural Activities, Mr George Frudenstein. It was now no longer a construction site but a centre for the performing arts — officially. And Sydney's establishment flocked around it with new enthusiasm now that the ball was in 'culture's' court.

The first major function came in July when The Australian Ballet Company's film of Don Quixote was premiered before a $50-each audience, including the Prime Minister. It was a prelude to the splendour of Sir Asher Joel's opening, still three months away. The champagne flowed, there were presents for all the guests (Estee Lauder perfume for women and after-shave for men) and the media gushed.

The media laughed — then was angry — when it was announced a few days later that 100 seats in the Opera Theatre would have no view of the stage. The Opera House management retorted that these seats would be sold to students who were there to listen to the music, or who wanted to follow the libretto or score during the performance. Or they could be sold to blind people at reduced prices. About the same time there was an argument over the Government's decision to pave the huge forecourt to the Opera House with bitumen instead of with granite slabs as originally planned. The argument was short lived: the Government refused to buy into it.

As it turns out it was probably a wise decision. The pink granite used on the broadwalk and the walls of the building would require almost daily steam cleaning to remove oil and rubber stains, had it been used on the forecourt. The first major test of the Opera House's ability to function as a diverse performing arts centre came in August when all four theatres were used at once and the critics heaped praise on the facilities — though there was and still is a deal of criticism about lack of space in the orchestra pit of the Opera Theatre.

Some performers were beginning to complain about the air conditioning, saying that it was ruining the voices of singers, for example. Others complained of the lack of parking facilities and threatened to boycott the opening unless things were improved. They also complained of high prices for food and drink. The public generally was complaining about the high price of seats for most performances.

The raking glass roof-wall of the harbourside foyer of the Concert Hall brings Sydney Harbour inside the Opera House.

The Concert Hall, a few weeks before opening night. Work on the organ behind the stage will not be finished until 1976.

Then came Friday, September 28, 1973. It was still a month before the Queen would be in Sydney to open the Opera House officially. But most of Sydney's opera and concert lovers saw September 28 and the days following as the opening of the complex. At last, there were public performances, the sort you could attend by buying a ticket at a booking office and just turning up — rather than by wangling a special invitation.

The Opera Theatre opened that night with a performance by the Australian Opera of Prokofiev's War and Peace. It was hailed as a masterful production and the company was widely praised for its handling of the difficult stage. The following night the Concert Hall was thrown open for the first public performance there — an all-Wagner evening by the Sydney Symphony Orchestra with Birgit Nillson as soloist. And then on the Sunday night it was 'people's night' with a performance by the all-Australian boy Rolf Harris. Champagne and beer flowed in the bars and there were few complaints.

The Opera House was into its first season but it was still not yet officially opened. As always in Australia — even with public lavatories in some country towns — there had to be the official opening. This was what Sir Asher Joel had been working on for nearly two years.

October 20, 1973

Sydney, as it does on occasions like this (if there are other occasions like the opening of the Opera House), went not so quietly beserk. The Sunday papers gushed with over-indulgent phrases as they reported on the opening . . . *Grand Opera,* said one. *Happy and Glorious,* it said elsewhere under a picture of the Queen and the Opera House. Another proclaimed: *Sydney has its day of glory — and the world watches.*

The television coverage had started hours earlier. And so had the ballyhoo. Cars were virtually banned from the banner-festooned streets of Sydney. Ferry services were cut to avoid interference with the thousands of pleasure boats that had massed on the Harbour and were to be an integral part of Sir Asher's spectacle. There were pop music concerts to entertain the gathering crowds on both shores of the Harbour. In their enthusiasm they were oblivious to the very real scare being felt by the organisers of some sort of attempt to destroy the ceremony and the Queen and the Opera House in one spectacular hit by the Black September Movement.

Security at the Opera House had been incredibly strict for weeks before the opening. Rehearsing members of the Australian Opera Company were cleared for security at their city headquarters, herded aboard a bus and driven with an armed escort to the Opera House where they were locked into the opera theatre until their rehearsals were over. They were then driven back to their city headquarters. This went on for the week preceding the opening.

Even after the opening, officials at Bennelong Point were refusing people permission to go into the bowels of the building unless it was absolutely necessary. On the day of the opening specially trained bomb-sniffing dogs combed the building. And police sharp shooters lined the city buildings overlooking Bennelong Point.

The Queen arrived at Bennelong Point at 2.45 pm — 14 years, seven months and 18 days after the first construction work began there. As she looked up towards the massive sails from the official dais on the courtyard in front of the building nine F-111 fighter bombers (once termed by Prime Minister Whitlam as 'the flying Opera House') swept past in salute at 480 mph.

In silence the crowd watched an Aboriginal actor, Ben Blakeney, portraying the ghost of Bennelong, climb to the peak of the Concert Hall roof to the beat of a didgeridoo and deliver a two-minute oration reminding them that on Bennelong Point 200 years before the fires of Aboriginal people had burned.

As she and the 15,000 invited guests were buffeted by a 40 mph wind the Queen made a short speech of opening before going inside the building to unveil a plaque commemorating the day. She made a short inspection of the foyers and halls and made her way fairly quickly, all the time accompanied by a gaggle of officials and journalists, to the Harbour end of the complex. More than 2000 small craft were waiting here for Sir Asher's coded signal, 'Anchors Aweigh,' for the much vaunted spectacle to begin.

As an army signalman relayed his command, the Harbour erupted. There was a helicopter flypast, fireboats blew gushers, small craft hooted, honked and wailed, flares went up, 60,000 balloons were released from an army landing barge and tug boats churned forward straining the huge red streamers between them and the two pinnacles of the Opera House roof. As the streamers parted, the Opera House was said to have been officially 'launched.' Beer and champagne flowed again.

Then at night there was a $60,000 fireworks display on the Harbour to precede the official opening performance. The Sydney Symphony Orchestra under resident conductor Willem Van Otterloo, with choir and soloists, performed Beethoven's Ninth Symphony and a specially commissioned fanfare, Jubugalee (another name for Bennelong), by the Australian composer John Antill.

The performance was not great but it improved as it continued. But the 2700 invitees were generally more concerned with being there to see the glitter and glamour than they were with musical excellence.

After all, the Opera House had been in operation for about a month. October 20 was a day for celebrating. And who can blame Sydney for going wild? Sydneysiders paid for it through the lottery; they suffered long pregnancy pains; the moment of birth was a time for ecstasy.

And while Sydney celebrated Utzon was 11,000 miles away, driving through Spain as a tourist.

Everyone wanted to see the Queen at the Opera House on the Sunday after she had opened it officially.

The Big Three

Eugene Goossens

Father of the Opera House, Sir Eugene Goossens, gave more to Sydney's — probably Australia's — musical life than any other individual. And yet he was drummed out of the country he had grown to love, shamed by a Customs offence.

On March 22, 1956, a year after he had been knighted for his services to Australian music, the tall, powerful conductor was caught smuggling what was then called pornography into the country when he arrived at Sydney Airport after a visit to London. Later, fined the maximum of £100 because the courts were outraged by the offence, he felt he had to resign his dual posts as permanent conductor of the Sydney Symphony Orchestra and director of the Conservatorium of Music of NSW.

Goossens **was** music in Sydney for nine years during which he lifted its quality to international stature from an inconsistent, unco-ordinated scene crying out for some cohesive force to give it strength and direction. He took up his posts in 1947 when post-war prosperity and the relief from the tensions of years of conflict were creating a mood in which cultural pursuits were to thrive.

Born near enough to the sound of the Bow Bells to describe himself as a Cockney, Goossens was a member of an incredibly talented musical family of Belgian descent. On his mother's side he was a direct descendant of Australia's discoverer, Captain J. Cook.

He was the third Eugene Goossens to become a famous conductor. His brother Leon was one of the world's greatest oboe players; his sisters Sidonie and Marie were renowned harpists; and his daughter Sidonie was a talented harpist. Goossens' grandfather went to England from Belgium aged 28, married a well-known dancer, Sidonie, and became first conductor of the famous Carl Rosa Opera Company. His son, Eugene II, also born in Belgium, took over the Carl Rosa from his father.

Eugene Goossens III was born in London on May 26, 1893, had travelled extensively and completed nine years of schooling by the time he was 13. He had been learning the violin and piano since he was five, showed some interest in chemistry and electricity but, he once said, was poor at mathematics. Around 1916 he had become a talented violinist and won a scholarship to the Royal College of Music where he stayed, undergoing the sort of training he said was the only foundation for a musical career, for five years. He later joined the Queen's Hall Orchestra and stayed there until he was 21 and had five years of professional experience behind him.

Sir Thomas Beecham asked him to conduct in the Beecham Opera Company and the young Goossens accepted. He worked with Beecham until 1923 by which time he had become a thoroughly experienced and highly regarded conductor and composer. He worked extensively throughout Britain and Europe over the next few years and became one of the most brilliant lights in a particularly strong cultural scene.

In 1923 he joined the newly formed Rochester Symphony Orchestra, in New York, which had been

Sir Eugene Goosens.

founded by the Kodak Company head, George Eastman. Goossens became permanent conductor in 1925. At this time he was spending seven months of the year in the United States and five in Britain, crossing the Atlantic by ship 38 times in 34 different vessels. Then, in October 1931, he became permanent conductor of the Cincinnatti Symphony Orchestra, the post he held until he came to Australia.

Goossens gave his first performance with the Sydney Symphony Orchestra as its permanent conductor on July 17, 1947. The applause was frenetic. On his fourth recall to the stage of the Sydney Town Hall, Goossens declared: 'I look forward to making this one of the conspicuously great orchestras of the world. I feel that with the material I have, I can do it.'

'Whether he achieved such a feat, impossible in any case to prove or disprove, is unlikely and, in any case, beside the point,' wrote the *Sydney Morning Herald's* music critic in a 1962 obituary.

The important thing is that he did succeed in making the Sydney orchestra a body of players of which the whole of musical Australia could be proud, and which could take its place without apology beside most of the long-established orchestras of Europe and the United States.

'In his nine years here he greatly lessened the time lag between overseas developments in music and their introduction here; a time lag which has unfortunately reimposed itself since his departure. The programs of his Sydney concerts, which quickly won a following so faithful that it is still a matter of privilege to hold an orchestral subscription ticket in this city, were of an adventurous and boundless variety in choice seldom equalled at that time in the major musical centres of the world.

'Sir Eugene's related and lifelong concerns with both orchestras and opera have left a visible, obtrusive and permanent mark on the face of Sydney.'

Goossens was a passionate, dynamic and extremely talented man both at work and at play. Apart from music, his interests and considerable knowledge extended from driving locomotives to philosophy, classical and modern literature, poetry, painting, languages. He was an excellent painter of watercolours and an expert in various aspects of architecture and archaeology, a talented photographer, an authority on contemporary ships and railways.

His pale blue eyes and tall stature, his quiet, deep voice, emphasised the authority and directness with which he approached every subject. He was unafraid to criticise and used the press extensively to publicise his ideas and make his points.

All this lent strength to his campaign for a permanent home for the Sydney Symphony Orchestra. He did not see construction of the Opera House begin but when he died in England on June 13, 1962, at the age of 69, he knew that it had already begun to take shape on Bennelong Point, the site he had selected for his great vision.

One of the massive pedestals from which the roof ribs radiate.

Joern Utzon

'The invisible wind works up the water forming the surface into waves, varying winds — varying waves, but always of the same character. The character, the style, has developed from a series of shapes in combination, all with the characteristics of water, waves — waves within waves — the wave that breaks, foams, etc. In my thought I mould the invisible space with geometrically defined shapes in combinations and when I have established the void I want, I freeze the situation in my mind. Because I have moulded space with geometrically defined shapes, the whole enclosure of the void is fully defined and the surface of the enclosure is divisible in a number of similar elements. These similar elements can be mass produced — and, when their relationship has been clarified they can be assembled like a big jigsaw puzzle in space. Everything that can emphasise this idea and operation must be shown, for instance, method of production, erection system, colour. Decoration and colour must be as organic a part of this complex as the white foam is part of the waves in order to achieve a complete and consistent character and style.' — Joern Utzon writing in Zodiac, the important architectural magazine.

Utzon was steeped deeply into architectural philosophy when he won the design competition for the Sydney Opera House in 1957. He was virtually unknown in Australia but was making a name for himself in Denmark and Europe, and had won a number of competitions. Most notable of his achievements were two special housing projects in Denmark which were regarded as breakthroughs in the field of low-cost, yet stylish housing.

But even at this stage he was becoming noticed as a young thinker. He lived with his family at Hellebaek, a small town a few miles from Elsinore (Helsingor), of Hamlet fame, where he grew up, the son of a noted naval architect. Utzon has often said that his boyhood in Elsinore, playing near and watching the castle which Shakespeare used to open his play, gave him the opportunity to study how a large building relates to its environment when it stands close to a vast expanse of water. He has also said that his father's job as manager of the shipyard at Elsinore enabled him to study the architecture and structural elements of large curving planes, such as those he devised for the Opera House. It was his knowledge of ship-building he said that enabled him finally to solve the problem of the Opera House sails; how to make them work and to stay in place.

Utzon lives again in Denmark. At the time of his win in the competition he was designing with a pair of Swedish brothers, the Anderssons, who lived a few miles across the water. Utzon often commuted the few miles by ferry from his home and office in Hellebaek to the Andersson's office in Halsingborg.

Utzon was born in 1918 and studied architecture at the Copenhagen Royal Academy of Art. It was here that his approach to the philosophy of architecture was awakened and developed. He graduated in 1942 and went to neutral Sweden, only a few miles from his German-occupied country.

Utzon with the earlier model of the Opera House.

The spectacular opening ceremony. The Queen and Prince Philip meet official guests.

In 1945, the war behind him, he went to study and work in Helsinki with the great Finnish architect Alvar Aalto, whom he regarded as one of his two great Nordic teachers. The other was Gunnar Asplund. After this he opened a private practice, for a short time.

In 1948 he was in Paris where he met Le Corbusier, the great Brutalist. At the same time he met and was heavily influenced by the sculptor Henri Laurens, who taught Utzon how to create forms in the air, to express suspension and ascension. The same year Utzon resolved to follow the footsteps of Corbusier who had, in 1910, made a great tour of Europe and Asia to explore the architectural philosophy of ancient civilisations and the life styles which followed. He won a travelling scholarship which took him to Morocco where he was struck by the unity of villages and their surrounding environment, which had been brought about by the almost total use of natural materials. He was impressed by the sculptural unity this created — even in high rise buildings.

A year later another scholarship took him to the United States and, later, Mexico. In the US he met the great Mies van der Rohe and spent a short time with Frank Lloyd Wright.

But it was in Mexico where a profound influence came over him. He was extraordinarily impressed with the architecture of the ancient Mayan and Aztec civilisations. In these he realised the importance of wide, horizontal planes; platforms so big they were almost plateaux. They were, he reasoned, a great element of architectural expression. They had their expression in the massive podium of the Opera House supporting the almost flimsy, sculptural shape of the roof vaults.

When he returned to Denmark Utzon did virtually no design work that was realised in buildings. But he did work at glassware and furniture. He worked on the ideas that had grown inside him during his travels and entered competitions, including that for the Sydney Opera House. He was interested in solving the problems raised by incorporating the spirit of the ancient structures he had seen into modern, new buildings. It is almost certain that these thoughts went into the design of the Opera House.

Later, Utzon confirmed much of the basic design philosophy of the Opera House when he visited — after winning the competition — China, Nepal, India and Japan. His drawings of Japanese houses express much of what he saw as the Opera House's sculptural function: virtually no visible contact between the roof structure and the horizontal platform on which it rested. One drawing of a Japanese house shows no contact at all between the roof and the platform, which he said was like a table top.

Drawings done about the same time show an influence on him of the relationship between clouds and a watery horizon. At this time he was still working on the Opera House roofs and this observation must have confirmed to Utzon the correctness of his roof shapes. Preliminary drawings of the roof vaults of the Opera House show this: there is no contact between the roof shapes and the platform on which they 'stand'.

Utzon has said of the platform: 'As an architectural element (it) is a fascinating feature. I first fell in love with it in Mexico on a study trip in 1949, where I found many variations both in size and idea of the platform. A great strength radiates from them.'

Of his use of the platform in the Opera House, Utzon has said: 'The idea has been to let the platform cut through like a knife, and separate primary and secondary function completely. On top of the platform the spectators receive the completed work of art and beneath the platform every preparation for it takes place.'

It is this great concern of Utzon's for philosophy of design that contributed towards his departure from Sydney before the Opera House was built. For in almost every aspect of the building he sought to incorporate what he saw as the ultimate in both design and construction. This, of course, took much longer to develop to plan stage than a building which worked within tried and tested methods of design and structure. It required expensive model testing. And it meant painstaking work by engineers. Utzon agonised over the Opera House and so did his associates and colleagues. But for political reasons — for expediency — a government turned the agonising into frustration. This frustration eventually led to his departure.

But despite the upheavals of the Opera House — and in many ways because of them — Utzon has become a world figure in architecture. The Opera House — whether he likes what was done after him or not — will always be a monument to his vitality, imagination and perseverance.

Hall, Todd and Littlemore

When Utzon resigned, Peter Hall, then a young man just returned from study abroad to work in the Government Architect's office, signed a petition which claimed Utzon was the only man technically and ethically capable of completing the building. A few days later — after he had accepted the offer to take the place of the Dane as the design member of the architectural panel — he said the situation had changed.

And that was that.

He was 34. The son of a postal inspector, Hall was born in South-western New South Wales, at Narrandera, attended the smart private school of Cranbrook as a boarder. He was an accomplished cricketer and debater. At Sydney University he captained the cricket team and graduated in both arts and architecture before winning a scholarship which took him abroad for two years of study and work. At one time, when away, he actually asked Utzon for a job in the Dane's Hellebaek office but could not stay long enough to interest Utzon in

The Opera House has, over the years, become a familiar sight to ferry commuters leaving Circular Quay terminals.

employing him. They discussed the possibility of a job over lunch.

When he returned to Australia, Hall joined the very talented and prolific Government Architect's office, one of the breeding grounds for a Sydney style of architecture that is often called the New Brutalism. Its adherents are admirers of Le Corbusier but, at the same time, are interested in using Australian materials which intimately relate to the Australian (or Sydney) environment.

The greatest influence of this group of architects has been in the up-market sector of project-built houses in Sydney. Hall was well grounded in organisation and management. He was good at his job and a talented designer. Because he was prepared to tackle the job despite the criticism he knew would be directed at him for it, he spoke to Utzon. He told Utzon he would rather not take on the job because he wanted to see him complete the Opera House. But he accepted when told by Utzon that the resignation was final. He still had some reservations about the job, especially the ethical question of taking over from the Opera House's creator. He was eventually convinced that he should accept after a long talk with David Littlemore at the University Club, and with Lionel Todd. Hall thought the Opera House was potentially one of the world's most exciting buildings and he was eager to begin work, once he had accepted the enormous job of design architect.

'From the word go, there was no other speed than flat out,' he told a newspaper. 'I was appalled by the lack of definition of our job. The idea was that we should complete the building in the spirit conceived by Utzon but we had nothing to work on. We had to start fundamental research. For the first two years much of our time was spent overseas.'

Hall's attitude towards the arguments over the Opera House largely helped to shelter the building from unnecessary bad publicity during the time he was in charge of design. Constantly aware of the media's search for fresh disasters on Bennelong Point he maintained strict silence about the project. This was in some contrast to his life style, which was quite flamboyant.

He smokes cigars and dresses well. He wears his hair at a fashionable length and, when he took over the job, was driving a sporty Jaguar.

Lionel Todd was 36 when asked to neglect his practice, Hanson, Todd and Partners, and concentrate on the Opera House, in charge of contract documents. Todd was trained at Sydney Technical College and in 1966 his firm was noted for its design of the School of Mechanical Engineering at the University of New South Wales. In contrast to Hall, he is quiet and retiring.

He has said of the project: 'I believe Utzon constructed something rather like a conductor conducts an orchestra — on impulse and feeling. Maybe this is the school that Utzon was trained in. Our own training was different; more regimented perhaps. I think we have done a remarkably

As construction neared an end, Premier Askin took a look at the building with Davis Hughes and Peter Hall.

economic job. There is no way you can enclose a building in glass walls on the cheap.'

Todd meets criticism of the Opera House interiors with this retort: 'If people want to enjoy a good aesthetic experience, let them come to the Opera House. If they want to relax, let them stay at home in a darkened room with a double Scotch.'

His work on the Opera House has left him an expert on theatre design — a distinction which he regards as somewhat dubious.

David Littlemore was the man of experience, aged 55, when he was appointed to the panel. His designation was site architect, in charge of supervision of the project. His firm, Rudder, Littlemore and Rudder, was noted for commercial work in Sydney. He says he knew nothing about the Opera House when he was called to the Government Architect's office to discuss joining the team. He had seen it and thought it a fine piece of architectural sculpture. But it ended there.

The offer came as a shock but it was exciting, though a little daunting. He asked for 48 hours to think about it but had decided to accept well before the 48 hours were up.

Littlemore is a Queenslander who was educated at Scots College in Sydney, Sydney Technical College and Sydney University.

He says of the project: 'This has been the result of remarkable teamwork and an all-pervading sense of pride among the workmen.'

Of the building itself, he has said: 'Utzon's contribution was the sculptural shape. There is such a terrific impact in the Utzon shape that I will forgive it for any failure for form to follow function.'

He believes the building to be as near to perfect as it can be: 'It has performed well. Acoustically it is an outstanding success and that was a difficult task.'

It Could Have Been Better, But . . .

In the sort of sweeping terms that have often been attached to the Opera House it would be fairly easy to call it a disaster. It would be similarly easy to call it a triumph. Both would be wrong. For the Opera House is like its concept — complex, difficult to understand. To reach conclusions about it is difficult.

Certainly it could have been better than it is.

But its ultimate form was in broad terms locked into it from the start. Once the project was started there was little that could be done to change it towards what people expected of it — the last word in performing arts complexes. What has been achieved is probably the best that could be achieved in the circumstances.

What Sydney has now, after 20 agonising years, is a good performing arts centre and one that reflects fairly accurately the mores of the city's cultural life. Symphony concerts have been given priority over opera. The opera has to share facilities with large-scale theatre productions in the Opera Theatre. And this marries pretty well with the figures revealed in a national survey conducted in 82 Federal electorates just before the building was opened.

The survey showed only three per cent of those surveyed had been to the opera in the last six months or so; six per cent had been to ballet, 11 per cent to a recital; 24 per cent to a theatre; and 65 per cent said they had no interest in cultural activities. For those 65 per cent there is the popular function of the concert hall as a place for pop music as well as symphony concerts. And there is the non-cultural function of the exhibition hall and a variety of quasi-cultural facilities provided within the whole complex.

Certainly, opera lovers have cause to raise the criticism they have. The opera theatre as it is now is not very big, the stage limitations discourage performances on the grandest scale and the orchestra pit is cramped. There are disappointments for many, especially those whose minds turn inevitably to plush and gilt when they think of the misnomer, Opera House. There have been early disappointments about price levels — for both performances and food and drink — and about the booking system. But these must be teething problems. When you consider the Opera House probably has a life ahead of more than 200 years, the time it will take to remedy these things is nothing. Future structural alterations might meet some of the aesthetic criticisms of minor points, like ducting and insulation which can be seen in the interior from some places. But basically, if you don't like the Opera House now you won't in the future.

Within the limits imposed upon them the team which took over from Utzon has given Sydney the best they could considering the limits imposed upon them. To search for scapegoats for the lasting criticisms of the Opera House — its cost, its limited facilities for opera and the time it has taken to build — is futile. Sydney has its Opera House and that's that. The web of personalities involved is too intricate and too interdependent to break and analyse and apportion blame.

Utzon's design was grand and it fired the imagination of the judges who chose it. In strictly practical terms it ignored the form-function argument altogether. But it was chosen as a monumental sculpture, housing a complex for the performing arts. Utzon has said he wanted to build something that would attract people, draw them towards it. He presented it as a sculpture and never attached more function to the exterior than as a building designed to draw people towards it — a building that was almost totally designed on the outside for aesthetics. And this in itself was a marriage of form and function.

Inside, Sydney has an Opera House that is functional first and imaginatively good-looking second. The interior design, especially of the foyers has as much respect for Utzon's concept as was possible within the limits of cost and time imposed upon Utzon's successors.

Personalities aside, it is possible to strip the history of the Opera House down to the barest thread of a story.

The view from beneath the potted trees at the Harbourside Restaurant on the Broadwalk.

The folds of concrete give a cave-like effect to the ceiling of the vehicle concourse.

156

From this view it became fairly plain that the building and all its troubles are the creation of politics. Joe Cahill's apparently good intention of providing Sydney with a vast and varied cultural centre had a good measure of political capital with it. He wanted to build an opera house for Sydney but he wanted the voters to remember that it was him and his party which got it going. When the building began to lag, costs mounted and personal relationships surrounding the Opera House deteriorated, partly because of Cahill's politically inspired rush to build without adequate planning, the then Opposition parties in NSW were quick to turn the project into an election issue in 1965. Having won the election they were obliged to get the building finished — even if it meant cutting aesthetic corners and taking expedient courses rather than the best technology had to offer. This helped to create the sort of friction which led to Utzon's resignation.

Utzon wanted to build the best and he wanted to take time to develop ideas that were at the far limit of technology's capabilities. This was frustrated by the politically motivated rush to complete the building. The problems he had worked on since the inception had been tremendous and the constant confrontation with problem after problem must have taken a serious toll on his demeanour. It took its toll on Ove Arup and his staff and the breakdown of relationship between Utzon and Arup and Partners, formerly such staunch allies in the battle to build, probably helped to put Utzon in the fragile frame of mind in which he finally called it a day.

He had largely overcome the daunting structural problems by the time the new architects were appointed but they, too, were subjected to enormous pressures. In them the Government had placed the responsibility of bringing the project to a happy and economic conclusion, quickly. They had their frustrations and their design problems, some of them as big as those faced by Utzon. But their overseers, the Government, were obliged to support them.

It is hard not to sympathise with Utzon. But it's equally hard not to sympathise with Hall, Todd and Littlemore. For all of them worked on one of the world's most challenging architectural jobs while constantly under an international shower of criticism. In a way Hall, Todd and Littlemore deserve a deal of sympathy because, while they worked for seven difficult years on the project, the Sydney Opera House will always, unmistakably be remembered as Utzon's creation.

From Utzon's point of view, though, the germ of an idea — a monumental idea — was brought to the verge of reality and then snatched away from him. For while he did resign of his own accord, he felt that the project and everything associated with it had become intolerable and the situation was not entirely, if at all, of his own making.

Out of the bitterness of it all however, has come a great building — a building that will give pleasure to thousands.

CAR CONCOURSE

BENNELONG
RESTAURANT
RECEPTION HALL
OPERA THEATRE
CONCERT HALL
BOX OFFICE
INFORMATION

WEST BROADWALK
EXHIBITION HALL
MUSIC ROOM
DRAMA THEATRE
ADMINISTRATION
HARBOUR
RESTAURANT

The commemorative plaque in the box office foyer.

HER MAJESTY THE QUEEN
OPENED THE SYDNEY OPERA HOUSE
IN THE PRESENCE OF
HIS ROYAL HIGHNESS THE DUKE OF EDINBURGH
ON SATURDAY 20TH OCTOBER 1973

THE HON SIR ROBERT ASKIN
PREMIER